ULTRA SUCCESS

An Insight Into the Minds of Some of
the Best Ultra-Runners on the Planet

ULTRA SUCCESS

AN INSIGHT INTO THE MINDS OF SOME OF THE BEST ULTRA-RUNNERS ON THE PLANET

ANTHONY ROGAN

LUMINARE PRESS
WWW.LUMINAREPRESS.COM

Cover Design by David Casey

Printed in the United States of America

Luminare Press
442 Charnelton St.
Eugene, OR 97401
www.luminarepress.com

LCCN: 2022900778
ISBN: 978-1-64388-883-5

To Beckie for all your continued support.
I wouldn't have achieved anything without you

CONTENTS

INTRODUCTION

It was October 12th, 2019, and my girlfriend was driving Jamie (my friend) and myself from the camp site that we stayed in the night before our first 50-mile ultra to the starting line. During the drive, we both looked at each other and both had the same thought 'this is a long way.' It was scary but also a weird and exciting feeling. After getting all my kit sorted and numerous nervous stops at the portaloo (which is always a pleasant experience), it was time to head to the start line for the 8am start. The ten-second count-down began, and we were all off. There were hundreds of people, all with the same goal of hoping they could endure the 50-mile distance for their personal gain. I trained hard for this event and felt fit and knew unless something went drastically wrong, I would finish. After several climbs and some good mileage in the bank, we were at the first aid station filling up on any calories we could get our hands on, guilt-free junk food is one of the best parts of a race. It was here that I remember looking at the people tracker that was shown on a projector on the wall and thinking that there had to be some mistake. Most people were shown on the projector to be there or thereabouts at the first aid station but there was one person that was way up ahead. I thought there is no way someone can be that far in front at this stage of the race, but I was wrong. I didn't analyse it too much after that, as I was focused on my own race. It wasn't until I crossed the finish line in a time of 15 hours and 49 minutes that I thought back to that first aid station. I told my girlfriend about the person who was in front, and she informed me that must have been the winner who crossed the finish line in a time of 8 hours 47 minutes and 7 seconds. I sat there for a moment bewildered; I thought I am fit and strong and was proud of my result but this I couldn't get my head around. As I sat there eating my food provided by the race clapping for others who had completed the gruelling 50-mile race, I couldn't get over that the winner would have been home hours ago with his feet up relaxing...and this is how the book began.

I enjoy reading and particularly running books and people's stories through running. Ironically, this book idea came about whilst out running 10km down the canals of Birmingham. I was listening to 'No map in Hell by Steve Birkinshaw' on Audible and thought of how interesting a running book can be, and yet it is such a basic concept. I love hearing about things that runners do etc and thought back to that race a year ago. I was wondering, what is different between these guys winning races to everyone else, as well as numerous other questions flying around in my head. Yes, we can read interviews in blogs, magazines etc about individual runners, but wouldn't it be great if there was a book with lots of great runner's stories all in one place, I wished someone would write that. I got back to my hotel room (where I was living at the time) all excited and started telling my girlfriend all these ideas I had after my run, which is something that happens often when I run. I get very creative whilst out running. Why do I need someone else to write that book? I can do it. A few weeks later, I had a notebook filled with ideas, people to contact and a plan of how I was going to tackle writing such a book. A year on,

I had over 30 responses from inspiring ultra-runners and what started out as a pipe dream now was going to be a reality. I wanted to create a book that other runners could take inspiration from and get an insight into top ultra-runners lives to see how they differ from the everyday recreational runner like myself. The book itself is a unique concept with it being in the style of an interview format with set answers and the individual runner's responses to these. There is nothing like this on the market in the running world, so I wanted to be the first and I hope that you find it interesting and easy read. There is something in learning about other people and their lives that is fascinating, especially the elite. The runners that contributed to the book were all asked the same set of questions. I wanted to do this so we could see the difference or similarities between how each runner handles the same situation. The goal at the start of the book was to receive 20 responses from runners but after months of contacting people, I am overwhelmed with over 30 responses from runners all over the world. Running has been a part of many people's lives because of its simplicity of it; grab your running trainers and off you go. No gym memberships or anything like that, but ultra-running as much as it is still running is very different. It is constantly growing, and people want to try and see how far they can push the body and mind. For many, marathons don't seem long enough anymore. The hours of training that you must put in to succeed at an ultra-race are a lot more than your average recreational sport. In most recreational sports, you can put a couple of hours into a week and still be able to compete but if you do that in this sport, you will be in a world of pain. Running 50 miles or any ultra-distance is no joke, you must prepare properly, and this is just for the recreational athlete. The top athletes are on another level, with them running hours upon hours in the mountains every week. This is one of my main fascinations with the sport. The sport is growing but for years, people have been running these distances, pushing their body to the limit but not gaining too much financially from it, not compared to other sports anyway, even now. Whether that will change in the future is to be seen. I think it is incredible that these athletes will train just as much if not more than many other sports and not have huge salaries like the other top sports; they are doing it for the love of running. I wanted to provide an insight into these incredible athlete's minds and lives. I hope anyone who is reading this takes great inspiration and education from this book just as I did. It really did change some of my perspectives on my own running. It helped me believe that you can achieve what you want if you are willing to work hard for it and never be afraid of learning from a situation that might not have gone the way you thought it would. The book provides more than just lessons in running, it has a crossover into everyday life and for that, I thank everyone who contributed and took time out of their day to help answer the questions. Keep inspiring and passing on the message that everyone can achieve greatness if they just believe it...Enjoy.

Krissy Moehl

When it comes to ultra-running, there is not a lot that Krissy hasn't done. With over seventeen years of experience racing ultras, she has one of the most impressive resumés in the sport. Over these years, she has completed over 100 races, including 55 female wins and 2 outright wins. Krissy has podium finishes in some of the most prestigious races across the world, including Ultra Trail du Mont Blanc, Hardrock 100, Hurt 100, Ultra Trail du Mont Fuji, and Wasatch 100. She also finished 4th female in Western States 100 Endurance run in 2012 in a time of 18 hours 29 minutes which is a personal best for her at the 100-mile distance. There are many other impressive results that Krissy has attained over the many years of her being in the sport. She now coaches other runners to help them with their own running goals and help them get over the finish line in their first ultra. She works with more experienced runners as well; however, she primarily loves working with people training for their first one. Her book 'Running your first ultra' is a must for any ultra-runner.

1. What do you love about running and how did you get into it?

I love where my legs can take me. I didn't know that was possible growing up and the trails that I could look at from where I grew up. I just always thought it was beautiful but now I am able to go and explore it because of the strength that I have in my legs and my lungs. Then I got into it, but I have always been a runner for as long as I can remember. There are pictures of me as a little kid doing local school races, cross country, I ran for High school college. In my junior year of college, I studied abroad in Ecuador. When I came back, the running retail store that I worked at had been purchased, I went back asking for my job back for my senior year and the person that had purchased it went on to create a hub of ultra-running in the Seattle community, so I was in the right place at the right time. Scott Jurek had just won his first Western States; these were the mentors that I grew up under. I was 22 years old, female when there weren't a lot of women in the sport and I just got sucked into this great group of guys that saw the potential I had, and I didn't want to get left in the woods, so I just chased them around and got faster doing it.

2. Have you ever had a 'did not finish' (DNF), if so, how did you react to it?

I had three in my career; one was in Colorado, I had been misdirected on the course, so it was looking as though I was finishing in three hours on a 50k which is ridiculous but obviously, I hadn't done all the miles and they wouldn't let me go back out and finish the course. The other one was UTMB in 2011, I would say that 'failure' is such a loaded question because there is so much that we can learn and turn them into successes if we deal with them the right way, so I don't see something like not finishing as a failure if I learn from it. What I learned from it was I got so excited about the training, I was over there 3 or 2 weeks early, I ran around Mont Blanc in like 3 or 4 days, stayed at huts along the way, so I was in awesome shape, and I should have just rested once that was done. The rest of the Americans came over and Chamonix Valley is a playground for trail runners, call it FOMO (fear of missing out) or whatever I didn't want to miss out on any runs, so I just kept running and really depleting my body so when it came to race day, and it was a cold wet year, I remember not wearing many clothes and getting to an aid station and my crew wasn't there and then I didn't eat enough food and I didn't have any reserves on board because I went into the race overtrained so when I made the decision to stop I knew that it was because I had made poor decisions leading up to the race and it wasn't just something in the race that wasn't going right. It was this long series of decisions that didn't set me up right where I was. So, I didn't feel like a failure it's just in the sense that it has really taken the joy out of the race for me because I was so overtrained. I do have clients that I work with and they can't let go of their DNFs. So, it is a good mindset to work with to understand why somebody would DNF and going into the race making the plan around all of it like is DNF an option, if it is, this is the option we are going to talk through, it is not going to be something that we regret afterwards. To do all that prep work so that no matter how far you are running, it is going to be hard at some point, so you must have all the reasons why you want to stay in it, know the reasons that are smart to just take yourself out, be mentally prepared that way. I get a lot of guidance like that going in; it was like—you start something, you finish it. I have been very averse to DNFs, in over 200 races, I have only had a DNF three times, and one was because I had been misdirected on the course. I set myself up to finish 99% of the time. The third DNF was a 50 miler that I went into injured, and I knew. I think it's mostly mental preparation. I know what I am capable of, so other than the race I went into injured, I would not start if I could not finish. I am a pretty conservative runner; I start off slow. I know where I am at going into a race, I know there are a lot of great ultra-runners in the world who just race all out from the get-go and sometimes they set phenomenal records and sometimes they blow up just as phenomenally. I have never been that kind of racer, less risky, I guess.

3. Who are your greatest inspirations and why (either in or out of the sport)?

My parents, primarily they are very driven people. They are not athletes by any means, I am definitely the black sheep of the family doing the athletics and running that I do but they have always been very committed to what they do, and I think that's a great example, especially in an ultra-comparison. I have been asked this a lot. The biggest one is just seeing people in their passion. Witnessing other people in their passion. A great story is we were surfing on the West Coast of Washington State. It is brutally cold, we were in full wet suits, the full hoods, and mitts. I am not a surfer by any means; it was the first time I had been out; I wanted to try it and came in when the waves started to die down. It took forever to peel off these wet salty wet suits, sitting inside drinking a warm coffee and we could see the ocean from where we were, and the woman that had taken us who was a very good surfer I could see her light up because the waves were coming back in. The fact that she would go and put that wet, cold wet suit back on and go back into that ocean and leave behind this beautiful hot coffee, I was like—that's passion. You see that in running races, that's why we get so inspired when we see people coming across the line whether they are in good form or not, they've endured the same. We find inspiration in people who are so passionate about what they are doing, they will do it no matter what.

4. Tell us something interesting that not a lot of people know about you?

I speak a second language, my major in college was Romance Linguistics and I don't think a lot of people know that or what it does. Linguistics is the science of language, how and why our mouths work a certain way and the history of how language has evolved. Romance Linguistics is the romantic languages, Spanish, Portuguese, French and Italian. So, I speak Spanish as my second language because of that reason. I lived in Ecuador for 6 months in my junior year of college. It was the coolest thing I did for myself. Especially as a young kid making the decision, my parents were not psyched at the thought that I was going. They've always supported everything that I've done but they weren't going to pay for it or anything, so I had to make it all happen. Still, I am so glad that I did, and it feeds the travel bug in me; I definitely have wanderlust as a serious character trait, so that was early testing of them. I went to Iran last September, September 2019. That was the first trip that I have taken probably in 15 years, that wasn't running related.

Beautiful people, such a great culture and community and people who are so welcoming and so interested in communicating with us.

5. How do you manage family or home life around running?

It's always changing. Managing it is communication, just talking through what's necessary. It is not a skill that I have ever been good at. It is a skill that I continue to work at, just being really aware of what I need and communicating that back to the people I live with or partnering with or however that unfolds. Being able to listen as well to their needs and hopefully collaborate, and I like the word collaborate rather than compromise. Compromise means that somebody is missing out or giving up something that they want, whereas collaboration is where both parties can create the end result that fits everybody's needs. My ultimate goal is collaboration and communication. Managing training, I am definitely all about consistency. I would much prefer to get out for 20/30 minutes rather than pile it all into the weekend. Our bodies aren't made to do that; our bodies are made to move on a daily basis. I definitely believe in rest days as well. I tend to schedule them so that I can look forward to them. Sometimes life interferes, so you can't get your run in, so I'll just switch things around. The quicker you can get to acceptance, the less energy you are going to waste.

6. What are your interests outside running?

Travelling (see above). Running is a big part of my world; I am a race director, I am a coach, I train, I have sponsors. I have a mini-Australian shepherd dog that loves to run so she keeps me active that way. But I love Yoga; I love cooking, I love reading, I love to learn through other people's experiences through reading and audible books. I am trying to write my own memoir, so by reading other people telling of their story, I can take different things from it where I connect with the way they told their story. I always have some sort of brain candy book going. I am a book person, so I won't read on a Kindle I like dog-earing pages and that kind of stuff. A lot of what I do supports running. Give and take right, so there are things that I'll give up so that I can run.

7. Do you have any race day rituals?

I was very superstitious in high school and I wore the same everything, hair band, underwear, I did laundry three times a week if I needed to because sometimes, we had races 2/3 days per week. I learned to let go of that quickly in the ultra-community. When I first got into the sport, my job was working for a foot wearing company called Montreal and I would travel around to these different races and show off shoes and let people try them on and demo them. And then put everything away and then I would go join the race and that's how I found out that I was good at the sport. I was brought into the sport to be this community person, an athlete coordinator and race sponsor but then I would just be standing around, so I decided to go try this thing and I would win races as I was going along. With that, having any kind of pre-race ritual, there were so many variables between travel, and the work that I was doing, where I was staying. If I was hung up on like having to wear the same pair of underwear, I was going to have a problem. So, I let go of a lot of those. That's been helpful, I think. Control the controllable, don't try to get so carried away with trying to control everything. I am a spreadsheet person, so if I could put life in a spreadsheet, that would be awesome. I try to do that with my races quite often, at least my mental state. I try to keep that out of the spreadsheet and just really be present on the day.

www.krissymoehl.com
Instagram @krissymoehl

Ryno Griesel

Ryno has successes in trail running, adventure racing, and mountaineering. I had the pleasure of interviewing Ryno through Zoom and he is one of the nicest and most positive people I have met. He has won the 65km Skyrun and broke the record of the Hobbit 100km mountain run after winning the race in 2012 and 2013. He holds the record with Ryan Sandes of the fastest crossing of the 220km (10,000m elevation gain) Drakensburg Grand Traverse in 2014 (Red Bull project) in 41 hours 49 minutes. Ryno also broke the record again with Ryan Sandes for the fastest crossing of the 1507km (70,000 elevation gain) crossing of the Himalayan Mountain range (Red Bull project) in 24 days, 3 hours, and 24 minutes in March of 2018. Ryno has numerous other records and impressive achievements, including various top-five finishes on the Adventure Racing World Series—racing all over the world.

1. What do you love about running and how did you get into it?

I was never a great runner at school, I am not generally fast. The distances at school were not far enough to justify my slowness. I have always had a keen interest in the outdoors. After school, I started climbing a lot more and I have always had to balance my professional career with my love for the outdoors then later with sport. I figured if I am running or moving faster between climbing routes, I can fit more into a day. I went from one climbing route to the other; you typically climb in the mountains, so now organically you are running in the mountains. That's how my running started. Running started because I wanted to save time. I love people, I love relationships, I have a massive passion for missions and reaching out to people. My dream has always been to be a full-time pastor. I was late to live out my passion in the business environment and in the sporting environment. The relationships of those people I get to run with is what I really love about running. Running is ultimately an excuse for building relationships with some cool mates and like-minded people. When you come to the bigger projects, you get to know each other so much better and get to build those relationships even deeper.

When you are running, you get to spend some time in your own head or with somebody and building those relationships. It forces you to be real with yourself, real with your partner and actually experience life in its rawness and simplicity, how it is meant to be. When you run, there's not too much you can do apart from unpack those thoughts and decide what you are going to do with them. Running is a tool, what I really love about it is how I grow personally. It is hard, running is hard, I have run since after school and it doesn't get easier. You might move faster but it doesn't get easier. So why do we do it? Because it is so real, and that realness leads to growth.

2. Have you ever had a 'did not finish' (DNF), if so, how did you react to it?

I have had DNFs in races, I have been privileged to not have any DNFs in my big projects. It depends on your goal when going into these events. When I do projects, I have a contract with myself, I know exactly what I am getting myself into and I am not allowed to quit. Quitting is not an option, even if you crawl, even if your legs fall off, when you do a project you finish, or at least die trying. A project for me is something completely different from racing. Racing goal is to be the best possible athlete and runner you can be, it is a science and sometimes in the race, you are forced to make a decision that maybe to not finish this race due to injury for instance, recover and do better in the next race. I have tried to avoid DNFs as much as possible in my life because it hurts like hell. Unfortunately, I have had some DNFs in races but because the overall goal of racing is to be the best possible athlete you can be, sometimes a DNF in one race saves you and sets you up better for the next race. You try to avoid it but sometimes you must make that calculated decision.

Whereas with a project, whether I am running in Nepal or the Drakensberg mountains in South Africa, the only goal is to finish. I don't allow it; it is not an option. In Nepal, I got frost bite on day four, tore the muscle out of my knee on day seven and still finished in 24 days because you set yourself some healthy boundaries beforehand and quitting doesn't fit into those boundaries for me in terms of projects. It is a personal contract that we have with ourselves. Not finishing hurts a lot more than the actual pain of the race but has unfortunately happened to me but in terms of the bigger projects, I never quit. The times I did DNF in a race, it hurt so much I would never like to do it again. Over a long career, it has happened once or twice. Two important things for me when having a DNF is allowing myself to feel the disappointment because ignoring it won't make it better but then get over it as quick as possible, get over yourself and get on with the next challenge.

The more you quit, the easier it gets. The more you quit, the easier it is to justify quitting next time and convince yourself. That is why I try special projects to not allow myself to even think in that direction. If it is 3 o'clock in the morning after you haven't slept in 6 nights, then there are a lot of good reasons to quit. A race is a more controlled environment, and it may be that the goal is to be the best runner in the next 6 months, then not finishing one race for the bigger cause is maybe justifiable. But the reality of not finishing is that if you quit in one race, it becomes easier the next time and easier the next time, up until the point where I might cultivate a 'quitting culture' within myself. I realised that and this is why I will always try not to quit. Unfortunately, over many years it has happened once or twice, but the reality is that you want to avoid it because it could easily become a habit even if it is just a habit in your head to justify why, 'it is better to quit now because the next race will be better.' When you are in the race, especially on a project, you are not capable of making those decisions on the go. There are just too many calculations and variables going. Ideally, you want to make those decisions before you go into a race, or before you go into a project, have a plan A, B and C. In a project, I only have a plan A; if I die trying to succeed in plan A, that's kind of it.

3. Who are your greatest inspirations and why (either in or out of the sport)?

My good friend Ryan Sandes that I do these projects with is my ultimate inspiration; he is a phenomenal runner, a great guy. He was my role model—and still is. He was my role model way before we started doing projects together. I followed his career, I actually went up and asked for his autograph, we got chatting and we realised there is actually some overlapping mountain passions, and we did our first Drakensburg traverse fastest known project in South Africa, which is the Drakensburg mountains in South Africa. We just became friends but the respect and the aspect of him being my role model and my inspiration will forever remain. I am just super pleased that I can actually do these and run with him as well. Ryan Sandes is definitely my inspiration when it comes to sport and how to conduct yourself as an ambassador for the sport.

4. Tell us about your greatest failure?

It is interesting because it all depends on what our definition is of failure. I will answer this 100% honestly, from my experience, because other people say that it is not a failure, but my Nepal project with Ryan running across the great Himalayan trail, 24 days, 1,500km, 70,000m of elevation. In my mind, that is my biggest failure ever. If you look at it from the outside, people say, 'it can't be a failure, you set the new record, beat it by 4 days, you ran with Ryan, you set a world record,' but for me, it was a failure because I felt that I had disappointed him. I had to make certain decisions early on in the project, I had to take my gloves off and sub -15/20 degrees to be able to read the map to get us out of a difficult situation. I knew at the time it was the best possible call. I knew I was possibly going to expose myself to frost bite—which I did, but that frost bite led to a downward spiral in my physical abilities, in my mental abilities. That became a really really tough 20 days following that. It went from bad to worse.

From the outside, people said;

'Well done for not quitting!'
'Well done for pushing through.'
'Well done for setting a new record.'

But for me, it's like I know I am better than that; I know I could have performed a lot better. I know that I am athletically a lot better, I am not on Ryan's level, but I could have been a lot better than I actually performed. So, in my opinion, that was a failure. I failed myself by not being mentally stronger than I could have been. So, my biggest failure is what other people would see as being my biggest athletic performance to date. That's setting a record on the Himalayan trail but to me, that has been my biggest failure. I would like to either go back to that project and re-do it for myself or Ryan and I working on some other projects where I would hope to apply what I've learnt better so that I can have a little bit less of a failure complex on how I performed in Nepal. The journey, the definition, everything is personal. That's what makes running so awesome, it's real and it's personal. What is great for you is not great for me.

I think it is very important that we are all clear of why we do things, because it's going to be tough, and then how do we handle these failures. You are not going to go through these journeys without failure and failure is not a universal definition; it's really a personal dream and journey and experience.

5. Tell us something interesting that not a lot of people know about you?

Due to the current times that we live in, a lot of people outside of your immediate circle really know you through media either from social media or general media. So, the first thing, very few people know that I don't run full time. Very few people know that I am not full-time in the sports industry. I am very actively involved with brands in South Africa, Salomon and Suunto and Ford. I work on projects with Ryan and with Red Bull, so people might assume that I must be a full-time runner—not because of performance just because I am so passionate about it—and then 'if he's not a full-time runner, surely the rest of his time is spent in the sports industry.' Which I do spend a lot of time in, but I would say that I spend about 10% of my time in the sports industry.

I am a qualified Chartered Accountant; I specialise in high-level international tax as well as mergers and acquisitions. I come from a suit and tie background; that's what I studied, that's what I grew up with. Apart from the pure accounting and tax side, I have got quite a few business interests in various companies worldwide. I would say that I spend about 80% of my time on corporate business as opposed to sport. The second thing that people don't know is that whether it is business or sport, I just use it as an excuse to build relationships. My biggest passion is to be a Pastor, to be a full-time missionary. I see the tools to build the relationships for a greater good. I am a Christian and my ultimate goal is to impact people positively, and I use both sport and business to do that in the best possible way that I can.

6. How do you manage family or home life around running?

I am personally very disciplined, and I don't sleep a lot. I actually extend my days as far as possible. My whole high school career, I basically woke up at 3 o'clock in the morning to study, and in school, I tried to do all the sport that I could humanly do. I wanted to be number 1 academically and I wanted to do all the cultural/outside activities of the school. I always had this thing of, if you live once—do as much as you can and if you do it, do it as well as you can. That is what has kind of translated into the rest of my life. So, I don't sleep a lot, and when I am awake, I am very disciplined but the ultimate success of all this—I am married to possibly the most patient and supporting wife in the world. I am married to Angela; we have pretty much been married now for 8 years. We got married quite late because, well, I pretty much travelled the world when I was younger. We don't have kids, so the time management is a little bit different from someone who maybe has a full family. I have a very close relationship with my parents and my two brothers, so we do spend a lot of time together. We all live in Victoria, in the same city in South Africa. I am very disciplined, but discipline without the support and the healthy relationship with my wife would have been nil and void. It's a little bit of all of that. I am known to be the most 'uncoachable' person. A lot of people have tried to help me with coaching. The problem is because I am so busy with so many other things, I had to learn to be disciplined but adaptable. The discipline is—I need to do and want to do something every day but to fit in a hill session on day one and tempo runs on day two doesn't always work. I try to do my training first thing in the morning, so I get up very early to do my training. I try to do two sessions every day so whatever I get to do in the evening is a bonus but if I can't get to it, then at least I have had that first session in the morning. I kind of train like a weekend warrior. I do some sessions in the morning in the week and then I go out and do some big distances on the weekend.

Even then, I don't tend to follow a plan as much as just be on my feet as much as possible. I'll disappear into the mountains for a couple of days on my own and really just enjoy myself because I discovered that if I enjoy what I do, then I actually move faster and harder and if I do that, I train better. I think to really love and enjoy what you do and have a passion for what you do and then find time to spend time on your feet is what's worked for me. It is definitely not a fool proof plan. I have a discipline to at least do something every day and ideally two times a day. How I then fit in those sessions that really depends on so many external factors with business, and a lot of my business is all over the world so different time zones. It is almost impossible to really plan it, but I try not to go to bed if I have not done something for the day. So today, I got up at 4/4.30 and I literally just sat on the indoor trainer because I know that today (Monday) business-wise is always crazy busy. So yes, I am disciplined in doing something every day, but I do allow myself some leeway in what I do for that particular session because I find that extra benefit of really sticking to a programme versus the mental baggage of being so upset with myself if I don't get to do certain sessions, it doesn't really add up. I have to make peace that I am not a full-time athlete but because I really love what I do, if I have a base fitness and just make sure that I do something every day and enjoy what I do when I am out in the mountains, then that has worked quite well for me in my sports career. Just enjoy what I do and have a good sense of humour.

7. What are your interests outside running?

A sport I did very competitively worldwide for about 15 years is adventure racing, where we run, cycle, paddle. Mostly three guys and a girl we raced all over the world, anything between 20k and 800-1,000km nonstop in one go. Through the sport of adventure racing, I have learnt I love cycling, any form of paddling, whitewater or river canoe, I come from a little bit of ice hockey background as well. Climbing, I love hiking with my wife and friends and just exploring the mountains.

One of my business interests is a group called Gravity Group Holdings in SA, where we have various companies training people that work from height. So, rope works and mountains in general are quite a big passion for me.

8. Do you have any race day rituals?

When I do the projects, I eat all the time, but that's not really a ritual it's just I need to feed. I am just constantly hungry. Although it's not a ritual, the reason I am saying this, people laugh at me. My backpack is always twice the size of anybody else I race with. People say they can't eat when they run, I can't stop eating and proper food as well, not just fancy gels.

In terms of a ritual, as I have mentioned, I am a Christian so whenever I do sports, I do believe in praying before we start running or start a project. And then, on a personal level, I just love praying when I run in the mountains because I just like experiencing creation, experiencing God's closeness running in beautiful mountains. I almost can't run without praying and therefore, if I do projects with Ryan or anyone else, when we start a project, we pray before we start.

The reason why I am sharing that, it's not so much that I feel that I need to pray in case something goes wrong, it's more running and my relationship with Ryan or whoever else I do these projects with is such a celebration of life that I almost can't pray and just say this is awesome and thanks for the opportunity. I am not someone who is trying to force my religion on anybody else, but I think just to acknowledge that what we do is a privilege even though sometimes it is hard, and my form of acknowledging that privilege to be able to be alive, to be healthy, to be able to do these things is praying. So, I would say my biggest ritual is praying.

Just acknowledging that, in a race, you could easily go in a negative spiral, 'why is this so hard?' 'why am I here?' but the flipside of that coin is to acknowledge that 1, it is a privilege to be healthy and 2, I chose to be here. I'd rather do these things with a grateful attitude than a grump attitude.

www.rynogriesel.com
Instagram @ryno_griesel

Damian Hall

amian describes his first half marathon in 2011 as life-changing. Since then, he has gone on to complete some of the world's toughest races and placed on the podium, including The Spine Race and The Dragons Back Race. He has represented Great Britain at the Ultra Trail Championships. Damian has completed the famous Ultra-Trail du Mont-Blanc (UTMB) four times and in 2018, he finished 5th, proving that he is amongst some of the top ultra-runners on the globe. In addition, he has set records with numerous Fastest Known Times (FKT) for some of the most challenging routes in the UK, including Pennine Way (260 miles) and Paddy Buckley Round to name just two. Damian is also an Innovate Athlete and a UK athletics coach.

Anthony Rogan

1. **What do you love about running and how did you get into it?**

I love it first because it makes me feel free and playful and it has taken me to some pretty places. Obviously, you get the physiological endorphin high which can be very addictive. To be honest, it has been life-changing for me; I ran a bit in school but preferred football. In 2011 I did my first half marathon, and it blew me away. I got really into it from there. I did my first marathon and ultra-marathon the following year. Four years after my first marathon, I was in the Great Britain ultra-running team. I got really carried away, a bit of a midlife crisis. I love the sense of adventure you can get with it; running in the mountains is exciting. I guess they are safe adventures.

When I was younger, I would have loved to cross Antarctica, but I don't want to be away from my kids for that long or do something quite that dangerous, so ultra-running is perfect for me, its adventure more than anything.

2. **Have you ever had a 'did not finish' (DNF), if so, how did you react to it?**

No, none of them, thankfully.

3. **Who are your greatest inspirations and why (either in or out of the sport)?**

In the sport, I am most inspired by people who are ethical as well as great runners. Dan Lawson, who is a GB runner, 24-hour European champion and he co-founded with his wife ReRun Clothing. Jim Mann is another one record breaking fell runner who co-founded the Future Forest Company and treesnottees. They have both used running and through running have made a big important ethical decision. In the US, Clare Gallagher is an amazing runner who speaks out about the climate and ecological emergency. Also, Lizzy Hawker and so many more. Lots of inspiring runners.

Outside of running, I would say Arsène Wenger the former Arsenal manager, I love his idealism, and stubbornness which is a strength and a weakness. I think he ultimately cared about people more than winning and trying to play football in a certain way which I admire.

4. Tell us about your greatest failure?

If it is in life, then it would probably be not working hard enough in school and getting some very mediocre exam results which did give me a kick up the arse and made me respond with wanting to show that I could do this stuff. I had some terrible A-level results. I didn't bounce back with loads of A's, but I got some better results and went to university and did a couple of degrees almost to prove to myself and others I wasn't as stupid as my GCSE and A level results made me look.

In terms of running, it was my GB debut where I had a nightmare with cramp; it was the first time I experienced cramp. I did finish the race but with a pretty miserable placing. It is a team score event so that affected the overall placing of the team, which wasn't great. It was quite embarrassing. A low point in my running. Putting on a GB vest and representing your country should be amazing and you're doing that on behalf of people you're representing and then to belly flop is humiliating.

5. Tell us something interesting that not a lot of people know about you?

I grew up without a television and don't really have one now. I went to a Rudolf Steiner school. My middle name is Alexander, and I am a cat person rather than a dog person. I am an Australian citizen. I played football very briefly for Forest Green Rovers youth team when they were much more rubbish than they are now.

6. How do you manage family or home life around running?

I have two young children, but I have got no social life. If I am forced to choose between socialising and running, I will go running. I think there are two types of runners, those that will get up for a 5am alarm and those that press snooze. You can make your own mind up which one of those I am.

7. What are your interests outside running?

I have been a football fan for most of my life, I was obsessed with football before being obsessed with running. I was a football journalist. I still follow football, but I don't go to games anymore I much prefer to go running. I still listen to podcasts and watch Match of the day. I support Arsenal and Forest Green Rovers. I was into music and film before becoming a parent, but film has been forgotten about as I can't stay awake for one now anyway. I love bands such as Radiohead and The Smiths.

8. Do you have any race day rituals?

Yes, rubbing Vaseline on my bathing suit area is one. Almost always try and have a good strong cup of tea or two. I always like to phone my family and speak to my kids beforehand, sometimes that's the night before. They nearly always wish me "bad luck daddy." That makes me feel more relaxed and I will want to speak to them like any parent. I will always try either the day before or the day of depending on the time of the race to have ideally an hour of not thinking about the race. Normally I get quite obsessed with things and it's good to have an hour watching a film or reading a book and just zone out. In terms of food and things like that, I am careful not to have too many rituals because when you race abroad, you might not find the food you want and that might stress you out, so I don't worry about things like that.

Damian also has a book—'In it for the for the long run,' published by Vertebrate Publishing.

www.Damianhall.info
Instagram @ultra_damo

Anthony Rogan

Fiona Oakes

Fiona holds numerous world records at the marathon distance, including being the fastest female to run a marathon on every continent with an aggregate time of 23 hours 27 minutes and 40 seconds. She is a proud vegan and is passionate about helping animals. She runs an animal sanctuary and uses running to try and aid animals. In 2018 she won her age group in the women's category (50-59) in The Atacama Crossing race, a 250km gruelling multi-stage race through the driest place on earth. In 2017 she was the first vegan woman (as far as she is aware) to complete the renowned Marathon des Sables (MDS). A documentary was made about the MDS experience called 'Running for Good.' In addition to this, Fiona has a book about the experience called 'Running for good—The Fiona Oakes Story.' All the proceeds go to Tower Hill Stables Animal Sanctuary.

1. What do you love about running and how did you get into it?

I love the raw, pure freedom running gives you. It's just you against you out there. Very simplistic—you can enjoy and embrace nature in all its forms, the terrain, the conditions, and the emotions. I started running to show that being vegan isn't prohibitive to doing anything—including the most demanding of sporting disciplines. It was before social media, so the only way you could get coverage was if you did well. The better you could run, the more effective the advocacy would be.

2. Have you ever had a 'did not finish' (DNF), if so, how did you react to it?

I have never had a DNF in either racing or training. My mental strength is my only 'talent', if you can call it that.

3. Who are your greatest inspirations and why (either in or out of the sport)?

Anyone and everyone who is out there—trying their best inspires me. If you want a name in sport, it is probably Haile Gebrselassie because he was so talented and yet so humble and showed me great kindness at many races, which meant so much as I very often felt alone in the presence of the world's best at races and on start lines!

4. Tell us about your greatest failure?

My greatest failure is not being able to do more for those that need help. There is still so much work to be done, change to be made, and suffering to end.

5. Tell us something interesting that not a lot of people know about you?

I play the bagpipes rather well!

6. How do you manage family or home life around running?

I don't really have any life beyond running and the animal sanctuary. I am creative with my training and very often run early mornings around 03.30 and late evening. I am busy all day, so I don't take breaks after runs—I just work different muscle groups outside doing the chores!

7. What are your interests outside running?

Outside of running, I love caring for the animals. I also love music—listening to and playing.

8. Do you have any race day rituals?

My race day rituals are just to be very, very prepared. I always lace my shoes the same way and have a lucky necklace of a horse head which my mum bought me when my first pony died. It always travels and runs with me.

Instagram @oakes.fiona
Facebook @fionaoakes

Anna-Marie Watson

Anna-Marie has a decorated career in the sport of ultra-running. She was introduced to running from a young age as her father was a fell runner in the 80's and 90's. Using this to her full advantage, she has accomplished some incredible feats in the world of ultra-running. In 2015 she finished 2nd lady in Marathon Des Sables (MDS) and 5th lady in 2018. MDS is one of the most punishing multi-day foot races on earth. In 2016 she was 1st lady at Cappadocia Ultra Trail in Turkey. In 2019 she was 1st lady at ULTRA X Sri Lanka Multi-stage (250km). There are plenty of other accomplishments to her name. She is also a coach, a motivational speaker, and in addition, served in the British Army for nine years.

1. What do you love about running and how did you get into it?

Drawing on my words captured in a recent interview for the 'Why We Run' project by Danielle in the Lake District in October 2020 ~ 'It is an unstoppable force, without running I don't feel like myself. It's a sanity check. It's something that I do every day; it's about getting outside of myself, getting outside of my head, getting connected to my body, and being a part of something bigger. I just feel more alive and free, it just takes me away. It's a form of escapism, very much from everyday life, that you kind of get stuck in your routines. The key words that come up again, and again, why do I do it? It's feeling alive and the freedom and it's feeling connected to myself and to something bigger than myself as well'. I admit there's a fine line between passion and obsession though I always think back to Vincent Van Gogh's quote, 'I would rather die of passion than boredom.'

Running is seemingly written into my DNA and I was helpless to resist the lure of the open trails with the wind in my hair and feet skipping over the earth. My dad was a fell-runner of the 80s and 90s, so the majority of my weekends were spent in the Lake District waiting for my dad to finish the Borrowdale fell race, Langdale Horseshoe, Coniston fell race, the list continues… and the May half-term holiday meant the annual pilgrimage up to Scottish island of Jura for the fell race. The Watson family calendar revolved around the fell racing season where my mother, my younger brother and myself were self-appointed cheerleaders. Several of these events had junior races, so it was natural my brother and I joined in the fun. It was far more preferable to waiting for my dad to finish! I've always believed my first ultra was the CCC (Courmayeur-Champex-Chamonix) in 2008 though during a recent lockdown inspired clear-out I discovered my finishers certificate from 'The Tour de Trigs' 50-mile event in 1998. Looks like my ultra-running journey started ten years earlier than I remembered! Since 2015 I've been lucky to compete on the Ultra Trail World Tour series taking part in events such as the Marathon des Sables, Lavaredo, Trans Gran Canaria and Ultra Trail de Mont Blanc. Alongside these endeavours I've also qualified for the IRONMAN 70.3 World Championships three times, completed two full-distance triathlons, taken part in adventure races and various other crazy endurance shenanigans.

2. Have you ever had a 'did not finish' (DNF), if so, how did you react to it?

The Diagonale de Fous will be forever etched on my mind as my one and only DNF—so far!! The race name translates as the 'fool's crossing' (!) sits as the most challenging event I've endured/enjoyed! The 100 miler snakes south to north across Reunion Island through dense jungle and ancient volcanoes where temperatures hit mid 30 degrees before plummeting to below freezing overnight. The route is extremely isolated, with endless knee-buckling steps and gnarly tree roots to test the legs and keep you alert. This ultra was my current nemesis after my first ever DNF in October 2019. I'd hoped to return to banish this monster in October 2020. This goal has shifted to 2021 courtesy of COVID-19 disruptions.

Anthony Rogan

3. Who are your greatest inspirations and why (either in or out of the sport)?

Every day I'm inspired by my coaching clients and athletes. It's a genuine honour and privilege to partner with them to work towards achieving their goals at work, in life and in sport. Their ongoing desire to improve themselves, whether it's managing remote teams, transitioning into a new leadership role, balancing the demands of work and life or training for their A race is a testament to their hard work, grit, and determination. I'm a massive fan of Gertrude Bell; an English writer, traveller, archaeologist, political officer, and desert wanderer. She roamed across the sand from Persia to Syria during the same period as T.E. Lawrence and is renowned as Arabia's 'uncrowned queen of the desert.' Her energy, intellect and thirst for adventure are truly inspirational.

4. Tell us about your greatest failure?

See my answer to Q2—DDF DNF

5. Tell us something interesting that not a lot of people know about you?

Running increasingly became a huge part of my life during my 30s though this hasn't always been the case. Most people are surprised to discover during my school career, I'd actively avoid PE lessons and remember my sports teacher writing to my mother with a warning to stop scheduling my piano lessons during PE lessons. Fast forward to my 20s, serving as an Army officer in the Royal Logistics Corps and living in Gutersloh officers' mess in Germany, my interest was in anything social as opposed to fitness!

6. How do you manage family or home life around running?

The concept of "managing" life and work around running makes me smile as running is an integral part of both. I'll admit over the last twelve months, my workstyle, lifestyle and running have been obliterated by COVID restrictions. The race season was non-existent, the majority of coaching work was cancelled, and I'm isolated from my family, who lives in Jersey and Chamonix. It's been tough and running has been my daily lifeline. I fully appreciate everyone's experience has been deeply personal, different and in all likeliness infused with pain. It's a confusing and messy space. There's no benefit or advantage to compare challenges or hardships. Pre-COVID, I organised my life around running, which can be a real challenge trying to fit everything in. Sometimes you have to decide what's more important, though with an element of planning in advance and determination, you can generally fit an early morning run before a family gathering or book a Bikram yoga session after a client meeting in London. I must admit I used to focus on the work/life balance challenge with some of my performance coaching clients and I would always learn (or re-learn) strategies through our conversations together.

Who knows what post-COVID or more realistically, living with COVID long-term will look like?

7. What are your interests outside running?

Beyond running, I've got a creative streak that emerges in a variety of different formats, whether it's crafting content for various collaborative projects with fellow coach Alex

Burn; so far, we've co-authored a chapter on 'Outdoor eco-coaching' in 'The Coaches Handbook' edited by Professor Jonathon Passmore and published by Routledge; crafting my latest blog post linking my passions of performance and coaching or designing semi-precious stone jewellery.

I'm a foodie at heart, so I enjoy discovering locally sourced produce; then rustling up tasty veggie goodies in the kitchen. Finally, I love spending time in PJ, I recently converted a Citroen Relay campervan. Simply parking up, opening the side door, popping up the hammock and watching the sun set is sheer bliss.

8. Do you have any race day rituals?

Race day rituals start before race day. Preparation is paramount based on the 7Ps of wisdom from CSgt Marriner, our tough Parachute Regiment Sergeant who had the honour of accompanying Zero Platoon through our officer training at the Royal Military Academy Sandhurst, which will be forever etched on my mind. I remember his gruff and direct manner as he uttered the words, 'Ladies, remember the 7Ps in every situation and everything will work out. Prior Preparation and Planning Prevents P** Poor Performance.' Sound advice, which I've followed ever since. Everything is planned out and triple checked with military precision the night before; picnic packed, kit laid out and support crew briefed. I'm a total duvet monster, so it's all about cramming as much sleep in beforehand as possible. In my last couple of races, I've adopted the ritual to write 'Be the tortoise' on the back of my left hand. It's a tactic that hopefully encourages me to start the race slow.

The Coaches Handbook link: http://jonathanpassmore.com/product/the-coaches-handbook/

Coaching Outdoors podcast link: www.coaching-outdoors.com

www.rfmcoaching.com
Instagram @rfmcoaching

Stephanie Howe

S tephanie has always been a runner, whether she liked it or not. She didn't enjoy running at a young age and it took until college for her to fall in love with trail running. Despite her lack of enjoyment of running from a young age, she has achieved some great results within the sport of ultra-running. She has numerous career highlights, including being the Western States 100 2014 champion and 3rd place in 2015. In a successful 2015 running season, she won the Lake Sonoma 50 miler (course record holder), finished 8th in Ultra Trail de Mont Blanc, and was runner-up in Way Too Cool 50km. She also received a Top 3 ranking from Ultra Runner Magazine, International Trail Running Association (ITRA), and Ultra Runner Rankings. She holds a PHD in Nutrition and Exercise Science awarded from Oregon State University. Stephanie now works as a coach and sports nutritionist.

1. What do you love about running and how did you get into it?

My relationship with running began at a young age. I loved being outdoors and pushing myself and running came most naturally to me. I didn't always love "running" in the traditional sense; I preferred team sports. But, as I got older, I realised that I was good at running, and it's more fun to do something that you excel at. Today I love the feeling that running creates. It's the most freeing feeling when I can explore trails and connect with nature. It's my favourite form of activity and I love running on trails. I don't necessarily love running for the sake of fitness/exercise; in fact, running on roads just to get in a workout doesn't really appeal to me. My reason behind running is to create that feeling of satisfaction and joy by connecting to the outdoors and running on trails.

2. Have you ever had a 'did not finish' (DNF), if so, how did you react to it?

If you are in the sport long enough, you are going to have a DNF. I responded to it just fine. I pushed my body as much as I could, and the finish for me that day was not the finish line. I think it's stupid to beat yourself up for not being able to cross an arbitrary "finish line" when your body is not able to do so. I don't mean giving up though- I never give up. I've walked in several races (hello UTMB) because I've had issues that weren't compromising my health. In that case, I do everything in my power to finish because I like to see things through.

Anthony Rogan

3. Who are your greatest inspirations and why (either in or out of the sport)?

I draw inspiration from so many people, including a lot of people that just adventure and don't give two sh*ts about what other people think. I like when athletes do things for internal gratification rather than external acknowledgement. That's rare among "elite athletes," and therefore, I don't look up to many of them as much. Runners that have inspired me in one way or another are: Anna Frost, Meghan Canfield, Rory Bosio, and Tonya Littlehales. I consider all of those women good friends and they have taught me so much about life beyond running.

4. Tell us about your greatest failure?

I don't see anything as failures, rather as opportunities for growth.

5. Tell us something interesting that not a lot of people know about you?

I was a softball player in high school and wanted to attend Arizona State to play softball. I was a pitcher!

6. How do you manage family or home life around running?

Running is just a piece of me. I don't revolve everything around running; rather running fits into my life. I have a newborn right now, so it's all about balance. I don't want to miss out on life and focus too much on one area. It's not healthy!

7. What are your interests outside running?

Cooking, eating, drinking wine, being a woman in science, being a new mom, travelling, and adventuring. I pretty much like anything outside and spend as much time as possible exploring the outdoors.

8. Do you have any race day rituals?

Not really. I just usually look forward to treating myself to a full day on the trails.

Instagram @stephaniemariehowe
www.stephaniemariehowe.com

Brittany Peterson

rittany is a professional ultra-runner who has competed and podiumed in many different distances from 35km, 50km, 73km, 100km, and 100 miles. She has numerous podiums under her belt, including finishing 1st female at Bandera 100km in 2019 and 2021. She has many notable wins at the 50km distance and a solid 2nd place finish at the Way Too Cool 50km in 2018 with a time of 3 hours 46 minutes 43 seconds. In 2019 Brittany claimed 2nd place at Western States 100-mile Endurance Run in the United States. Some said that she was kind of an underdog for this race as she didn't have much national recognition for the 100-mile distance. She also became the fourth-fastest woman in the races 45-year history that day. Racing aside, Brittany also broke the record for the fastest known time (FKT) for climbing all nine of Idaho's 12,000 feet peaks in a time of 36 hours and 44 minutes. She is also an Occupational Therapist managing a full-time career around her running and loves spending time with her dogs.

1. What do you love about running and how did you get into it?

I grew up next to a state park and my high school cross country/track coach was a strong influence in trail running and just adventuring and making running fun. One of my fondest Saturday runs was basically going deep into the state park, getting off trail and running all along a creek, wading waist-deep to ankle deep as we literally ran in the water for miles. It was a great way of just having fun and not thinking about running, while at the same time, getting a great workout in and enjoying the company of like-minded people. Now, I really love several aspects of running. The ability to test your mind and spirit, the accomplishment after a hard push, whether it is in a race or after a workout, the adventure of discovering new trails or tagging peaks, etc.

2. Have you ever had a 'did not finish' (DNF), if so, how did you react to it?

I have not had a DNF. I have a strong philosophy of finishing what I start. However, I do respect that there are times that it is smarter to DNF and not worsen an injury, etc. That being said, I respect when runners who are having a less than ideal day stick it out and finish. Especially when that person is an elite athlete and, as my coach says, "finishes with the mortals." It shows all of us that we can have less than ideal days and that things can go wrong, which makes our sport very unique and challenging. But, finishing in these circumstances shows dedication to the sport and respect for the challenges that everyone faces. It is a way for everyone to connect, as a runner, as a human and overcome or deal with adversity. I haven't had my turn when I've had to make a tough call and DNF, and I hope not to. But I have had a 20+ mile walk of shame where I finished in a time and place that was under my potential. I so badly wanted to DNF, but that was the true "easy way out." It was satisfying to still finish and face that adversity head on, which ultimately made me stronger and made me far more appreciative of the days that go well.

3. Who are your greatest inspirations and why (either in or out of the sport)?

As I was an up-and-coming elite, I had so many strong women in the sport to look up to. I love and appreciate the women who have paved the way in this sport—Ida Nilsson, Megan Kimmel and Courtney Dauwalter are the few that always come to mind. Strong, humble, genuine people. These women represent integrity, teamwork, positive body image and all-around badassery.

4. Tell us about your greatest failure?

I can certainly think of races and poor performances as a "greatest failure," but I want to expand beyond just running. I think there are many people talking now about linking self-worth to running. I don't look at this as a failure, but I look at this as an area that I want to improve (and have been working on improving). Running is such a personal sport and many of us find an escape with running. I have found, both pre-professionally and as a professional runner, that I link my self-worth to my running performance. This is a very huge challenge and leads to many pitfalls such as depression, overtraining, injury, eating disorders, etc. I think in my running performances, my greatest "failures" (i.e. poor race performances) actually lead to my greatest growth. Challenging the evils of comparison, finding the true sources of my self-worth, monitoring balance and healthy relationships with social media avenues. These have all been the results of the greatest lows that can come with perceived failures, as well as the identity crisis that can occur with injury or aging as an athlete. I'm certainly only in the beginning of this journey but I have found great growth, improvement, and more happiness as I've reframed "failures" and find my true self-worth as a runner, but also as an individual who has many great attributes.

5. Tell us something interesting that not a lot of people know about you?

I was a mediocre runner in high school and college. I went to a D3 college that had a good Occupational Therapy program and had ice cream in the cafeteria. I think this was actually advantageous, as it further developed my love for running and my bond with people through running. I came out of college without significant running burnout and was able to further build and develop as I discovered my niche with running. I think this is a cool story because there are so many elite athletes are decorated collegiate athletes, but not all have this background. It can be inspiring that there may be talent and skill that you can develop and capitalize on years later in life, even if you were a mid-packer or even a non-runner back in the glory days!

6. How do you manage family or home life around running?

I am very fortunate to have a partner who is also a professional runner (Cody Lind). We have a good system of communication and respect for each other's training. We do many of our runs or trips together but also do much of our running separately. We balance the home responsibilities and at times take turns running while the other crews during an important long run (which also compliments giving the dogs attention!). I work full-time as faculty at a university, which also builds in boundaries for improved balance between my different passions in life. It also helps reduce over-training, as I have several responsibilities to manage.

7. What are your interests outside running?

I am an Occupational Therapist and have worked in neurological rehabilitation for the bulk of my career (10+ years), with the last 3 years being in an academic setting, which has allowed greater pursuits as a professional runner and greater ease for traveling and competing, as well as training. I am very passionate about teaching and love teaching about stroke, brain injury and spinal cord rehabilitation. Other interests are being with family and friends, backpacking, mountain biking, rock climbing, being with my dogs, gardening, and house projects.

8. Do you have any race day rituals?

I always get up 2 hours before the start (at least). Eat breakfast—bagel with peanut butter and banana at this two-hour mark to make sure I've properly digested the food and to keep my stomach happy. Pre-race dinner is usually pasta—fettucine alfredo with chicken, broccoli and mushrooms is my favourite. I'm the Type A personality that likes to be at the race start at least an hour early "to get nervous, so I can use the bathroom." I generally get a favourite pair of socks and wear those socks for every race, as well as the ponytail braid.

Instagram @runhappyb
www.brittanypetersonruns.com

Hanny Allston

Hanny has some huge achievements in orienteering, sky running, ultra-running, and a bunch of fastest known time records (FKT). She has accomplished international honours becoming a world champion in the sport of orienteering in 2009 in Taiwan. In 2014 and 2015, she was named orienteering Australian athlete of the year. In ultra-running she finished 2nd place in Ultra Trail Australia 100km in a time of 10 hours 13 minutes in 2017. She also won Ultra Trail Australia 50km in 2016 in 5 hours 10 minutes. Some of her FKTs are more than impressive. In 2020 she completed the Western Arthurs Traverse (Scotts Peak Dam Return), Tasmania solo and FKT in 10 hours 30 minutes. This route consists of 59km and a 3763m climb. In 2019 she finished the gruelling French Pyrenees Mountains solo traverse consisting of 19 days, 700km+, and 45,000m+ vertical gain. Hanny has many more endurance feats to her name. Just for the record, she ran a marathon in New Zealand in 2 hours 43 minutes.

1. What do you love about running and how did you get into it?

I love how it exposes you to the wilder outdoors as well as the simple moments of the day that might otherwise pass you by. For me, running is a window into landscapes, people, cultures, places and also myself. On the latter note, I find it has helped me to find my most authentic self and to be able to walk, or run, comfortably and proudly in my own shoes. I don't say this because of the things I have achieved in running, but rather I think that the experiences I have had, particularly more recently on my own solo and wilder trail running adventures, have helped me to realise, 'ah, this is who Hanny is when she is the best version of herself!' I don't think we can get to this point straight away, but rather it is an accumulation of many experiences over time, experienced with absolute presence & humility when we finally realise that we have found our feet... for now!

I got into running as a side to my elite swimming endeavours and then later as a way of training for an international orienteering competition. I discovered that to be the best orienteer in the world, which was a huge goal for me in my late teens, you also had to be the best runner in the world. I initially ran on trails, learning from old-timer trail runners here in Tasmania, but over the years, I found myself competing in a wide variety of running events, from trail to ultra, track athletics to the marathon. It has only been in the last 5 years or so that I have returned to the trails where I find my happiest, most playful self.

2. Have you ever had a 'did not finish' (DNF), if so, how did you react to it?

For sure! We have to realise that a 'did not finish' is not a failure, but exactly what it says—I did not finish. These moments are here to help us learn what we can do to enhance our performance for next time and even to sometimes realise worlds in which we no longer belong...where the flame or love has died. If we only ever succeeded, we would truly miss out on these valuable learning experiences.

The same was true for my orienteering. I am absolutely certain that the two reasons I became a world-class orienteer was through: learning to dig deep into my mistakes and discover the true reason behind them; and also my willingness to lean into discomforts to become a better athlete. The two questions I ask myself after a setback are: *Why?* And *What If?* I find these really helpful in uncovering what I can change next time to get closer to my dreams.

3. Who are your greatest inspirations and why (either in or out of the sport)?

I am so inspired by the quiet achievers who have an incredible capacity to play & perform wilder. For example, Tasmanian runner Stu Gibson ran the hugely remote and rugged South Coast Track here in Tasmania in an epic 9hrs10mins (92kms). I also find the likes of American photographer Jimmy Chin or freeclimber, Alex Honnold hugely inspiring. I love how they are committed to excellence whilst living the life that brings them greatest energy. These guys are all chasing their most authentic selves and thriving because of it.

Finally, I have been inspired by past coaches such as Max Cherry and Jackie Fairweather, who encouraged me to chase big dreams and taught me a wealth of lessons along the way. I am truly grateful for meeting them and I felt their loss terribly. Then there is my husband, Graham, who traverses life with humility and focuses on living authentically and wildly playful. I think it was through his encouragement and guidance that I found my wilder feet.

4. Tell us something interesting that not a lot of people know about you?

In 2017 I announced that I retired from competitive sport. I think a lot of people thought that I had hung up my shoes. But I think since then, I have achieved some of my proudest moments with my running, such as my 2019 solo traverse of the GR10 Trail across the French Pyrenees, a distance of over 700km with 45,000m of vertical climbing in 19 days. I've also completed some huge and wild solo 'missions' here in Tasmania, including the 65km Western Arthurs Traverse. I don't do these adventures 'to be seen' but rather to see the world and landscapes that inspire me. On both of these mentioned adventures, I really realised that my running is not just a physical challenge, but rather a combination of physical with mental, emotional and even spiritual elements. I love that I can walk into my 'athletic retirement' even more inspired than ever!

Now pregnant and weeks away from welcoming our first child into our family, I am excited to see the world through even more childlike eyes. To raise our little one outdoors as much as possible and include him in my own and my husband's dreams is the next exciting challenge. I am really looking forward to this adventure about to start.

5. How do you manage family or home life around running?

I have learnt that to be the best version of me and ready to engage with others and the busy modern world, I need to begin every day with 'me time.' That is, I always start every day off outside, even if it means getting up earlier before the world awakes to create this space for myself. I don't necessarily have to be running, but I just need to be outside and watch the world awaken. I always return home eagerly awaiting the rest of the day and ready to devote the energy I gained outdoors to others, my work, and the rest of the day's tasks. My husband and I are now discussing how to prioritise these important times going forward into parenthood so that we can both feel proud of parenting from our 'best shoes.'

6. What are your interests outside running?

Wide and varied! I was taught from a younger age that having a choice equates to a feeling of freedom. So, it has been really important for me to maintain a large array of things that make my toes tingle—hiking, riding, swimming, yoga, meditation, art, writing, running our business, travelling, reading, cooking… I always feel like there is never enough time in the day! However, I am very aware that the world needs a stop button. We cannot always expect ourselves to be on 'go mode' all the time. Therefore, the addition of writing, art, meditation, yoga, and quiet time has been a really important part of my athletic evolution, as well as for me as an adult… as Hanny.

7. Do you have any race day rituals?

When I was racing, I always started the day off like any other day. I would get up really early and go for a short jog outside to find myself and with it, a sense of tranquillity. Then back to the accommodation for a hot shower, a light munch, and a cup of tea. I found that if I neglected this everyday ritual, then I didn't feel like the best version of myself standing on the start line. Today, when I coach and assist others, I always recommend that they start the day empowered. Whilst this may require a different approach to mine, I do find that getting outside and earthing those nerves can really help to feel alive and confident on the start line.

Memoir (published May 2020)—Finding My Feet: My Story (https://www.hannyallston.com.au/finding-myfeet.html)

The Trail Running Guidebook (first published 2017, republished May 2020) - https://www.hannyallston. com.au/trail-running-guidebook.html

The Find Your Feet Podcast - https://www.hanny-allston.com.au/podcast.html

Blog - https://www.hannyallston.com.au/blog
Homepage - https://www.hannyallston.com.au
Facebook - https://www.facebook.com/hanny.allston
Instagram - https://www.instagram.com/hanny.allston/

Anthony Rogan

FOOD FOR THOUGHT

Ultra-marathon participation is increasing worldwide. It could be assumed that everyone entering a race or event wants the best possible chance of finishing. There have been several studies cited about whether your size increases or decreases your chances of completing an ultra-marathon. Studies led by Beat Knechtle (1) at the University of Zurich in 2013 suggest it might. The study consisted of 17 participants during a multi-stage race split over 5 days. The competitors were weighed, measured, and examined before the race. The researchers then recorded the finishing times of each competitor and used this information to decide whether variables such as height, weight and body fat percentage would be a good prediction of race success. Most measurements are taken, including height and body fat percentage, showed no relationship with the competitor's finishing times. Interestingly however, higher body mass and having a large upper arm circumference were both linked with slower finishing times. The findings from this study are not surprising; it does however mean that you might need to be careful when stacking on upper body muscle if you want to have greater success in ultra-running. It should be noted that calf or thigh circumference was not linked to slower race results. A further study published by Beat Knechtle (2) and his research team found similar findings during a 750-mile race over 17 days in Germany. This study used similar protocols to determine the results. This time the study identified that only upper arm circumference predicted the competitors finishing times and not body mass. The other factors measured were not related with finishing times in this study either.

Camelia Mayfield

Camelia has over a decade worth of experience in competitive running. She has competed and podiumed at distances ranging from 5km to 100 miles. Camelia grew up running in the hills of the Rogue Valley in Southern Oregon. With one of her earliest memories being camping whilst her father competed in ultra-marathons, it was part of her family's culture. Her running CV speaks for itself with numerous wins on some of America's toughest endurance courses. She has placed 7th and 5th at the Western States 100 in 2018 and 2019. She placed 2nd at the 2020 Javelina Jundred 100-mile race in Fountain Hills, Arizona. She has had great success in the 100km distance as well, placing 1st female at Waldo in 2017 and 4th at Bandera also in 2017. In the 50km Camelia has finished no lower than 8th place in the six races she has competed in, winning the Three Sisters Skyline in 2019 and 2020 and no wonder with a personal best marathon time of 2 hours 42 minutes 55 seconds.

1. What do you love about running and how did you get into it?

For me, running is a time of connection. I find myself building a lot of community around it and also a lot of connection with my physical sensations and my surroundings. It is a time when I can disconnect from other aspects of my life and live more "at the moment." I started running at a young age, as it was part of my family culture. Some of my earliest memories include camping while my dad raced ultramarathons or running events at the local All-Comers track meet. I was too stubborn to wear tennis shoes in the summer, so I would run the races in my Saltwater Sandals. I then started running cross country in middle school and it just continued from there.

2. Have you ever had a 'did not finish' (DNF), if so, how did you react to it?

I actually don't think I've ever had a running DNF! Maybe I'm just way too stubborn. I have definitely had to take breaks from racing due to injury, but I have been fortunate to go into most running races feeling physically and mentally prepared. I did have a DNF in a high school Nordic Ski race and that was a really bad feeling. I felt defeated and ashamed. I had no reason to quit other than the fact that it was a two-loop course, and I was struggling with form and felt like I was going too slow. Looking back, I see that it was a good reminder that I needed to humble myself to a steep learning curve.

Although I haven't DNF'd any running races, I think I have learned much more from races that I have finished despite slowing down considerably. Specifically, I went out way too fast at the Chuckanut 50k in 2018. In the second half, I was passed by at least a half dozen runners. I felt like I wanted to give up but knew that I should at least get in a good long run and just try to keep a positive mindset. About a month later, I placed 3rd at Lake Sonoma 50 miles and got an entry to the Western States 100. It was a good reminder to use "failures" as an opportunity to improve.

3. Who are your greatest inspirations and why (either in or out of the sport)?

I don't really have any idols that come to mind. Obviously, there are people in the sport who I find impressive, but honestly, I think I take the most inspiration from people I know personally. At the end of the day, my family has been so supportive of my journey toward ultra-running and the sacrifices that I make to get out the door for training runs and travel for races. When I really need inspiration during a race, friends and family definitely come to mind and knowing how much they believe in me. I also find a lot of inspiration in the athletes I coach. Being a mentor to them motivates me to be on track with my own goals.

4. Tell us about your greatest failure?

I can't really call to mind any specific event that I consider a failure. I think that a lot of my resiliency in the sport and my personal life has stemmed from being able to reframe things that are disappointing as something that I have actually grown from. One such instance was when I was 19; I decided to transfer from one undergraduate college on the East coast of the USA to one closer to home in Oregon (West coast). In some ways, this felt like I was "giving up" on spreading my wings and being more independent from my family. That experience was the first time I sought counselling, as I was having a lot of difficulty with making the decision for myself. There were a lot of unknown factors to transferring schools that scared me. In the end, the transfer provided me with many opportunities that I would not have even fathomed, most notably competing at a high level in track and eventually earning a scholarship. However, in the transition period, I was really having a hard time trusting my own intuition and decision-making.

5. Tell us something interesting that not a lot of people know about you?

I work night shifts as a social worker in my local emergency department. Not super interesting, but I have a lot of interesting stories as a result!

6. How do you manage family or home life around running?

I do my best to plan but also remain flexible around that! I get a lot of anxiety if I don't have a clear idea or general schedule of what I need to do in a day, so before I fall asleep, I will often make a list of my goals for the next day and events that I have scheduled. Communication with my partner is key for him as well! Most of our arguments centre around unclear expectations of how I am spending my time and prioritizing time as a family, so I try to communicate my daily goals/schedule as much as I can.

As far as managing home life, I find that meal-prepping and weekly grocery shopping is essential! This takes a lot of stress off my plate during my work week. I get really hangry when I don't eat, so it helps to have snacks and meals ready. I think that falling into a routine is also key. I know that I won't have the energy to do much on my long run days, so I plan for some of the household chores on other days of the week. I also am not too "type A" about if things get a little messy, which definitely helps me keep my stress down.

7. What are your interests outside running?

I like to cook, play with my dog, and Nordic ski. I work full time as a social worker, and I love working in mental health.

8. Do you have any race day rituals?

Eat a good breakfast, drink coffee, and hopefully poop! Most ultramarathons start so early there isn't time to do anything else. I lay my clothes and gear out the night before to make sure I'm not missing anything.

Instagram @cameliamayfield

Bongmusa Mthembu

B ongmusa is the epitome of determination and hard work. Before his running successes, he was working for a construction company as a bricklayer and cement mixer. At this point in his life, he was only running for fitness. After a while, he started entering races and before he knew it, he won the 2005 Maritzburg Marathon. His results speak for themselves, but it shows that dedication and consistency pay off. He has won Comrade's marathon three times and was 2 Oceans marathon champion in 2019. It took him several years before winning any ultra-distances. Bongmusa's first Comrades marathon seen him finish in 54th place in 2006 with a time of 6:25:19. That is a huge time difference compared to his personal best in the 2018 Comrades marathon, with a time of 5:26:34. It is madness to think that he only started running for fitness after all his accomplishments. Bongmusa also holds the South African 100km record running the distance in a time of 6:24:05. This had previously been held by Bruce Fordyce (also mentioned in this book) since 1989. Bruce is another Comrades legend. Comrades is a huge spectacle in South Africa. Bongmusa placed 2nd in 2016 and 3rd in 2018 in the World 100km Championships. It was 2016 in Spain where Bongmusa broke the South African 100km record.

1. What do you love about running and how did you get into it?

I first got into running as a way of trying to get fit. I like it because it helps keep me strong and healthy. It helps build confidence and improves my self-respect.

2. Have you ever had a 'did not finish' (DNF), if so, how did you react to it?

I have had this happen to me before. It was hard for me to recall what had happened during the race that I had a DNF. It was the 2013 Comrades marathon. It wasn't until I saw a video of the race that I realised what had happened and I was trying to think back to how my state of mind was two or three weeks before the race. I had to attend sport psychology sessions to help with overcoming what happened. I had to let my emotions out and go back to the drawing board. The year after, it was very emotional after winning the same race then I didn't complete the year before. I first won the Comrades marathon in 2014. In September 2014, I also lost my Fiancé.

3. Who are your greatest inspirations and why (either in or out of the sport)?

My greatest inspiration is my mother; I saw her raise us on her own. My father passed away in 1997. She is hard-working, persevering, and very independent.

4. Tell us about your greatest failure?

The 2013 DNF at Comrades marathon was difficult to accept. I was very emotional after such a long preparation for the race. I didn't know what would happen next. I had to face all kinds of questions. How am I going to face the world? How to face the people who love you? How to revive myself? The following year I won Comrades for the first time.

5. Tell us something interesting that not a lot of people know about you?

People don't know that I love laughing and I can laugh loud. Also, being a Zulu boy, we have a dance that's called Zulu dance and I love and enjoy it.

6. How do you manage family or home life around running?

Live simple. My family knows very well running is everything to me and they have seen how running has changed our lives. They respect me running a lot and support it thoroughly.

7. What are your interests outside running?

My interests are hiking and spending a lot of time with family and friends.

8. Do you have any race day rituals?

I do pray a lot throughout my running season.

Instagram @bongmusamthembu
Facebook @bongmusamthembu
Twitter @bongmusamthebu

Bruce Fordyce

Bruce is a legend of one of the most famous ultra-races in the world—Comrades. He is the most accomplished Comrade's runner in history, winning the race nine times. Eight of his wins were consecutive and in 1985 and 1987, he remarkably achieved the same time. After speaking to Bruce on the phone about his contribution to this book, you can hear how passionate he is about Comrades. For three years running, he won the London to Brighton ultra-marathon. In this event, he broke the world record of running 50 miles in a time of 4 hours 50 minutes and 51 seconds; he held this from 1983 to 2019 when Jim Walmsley managed to beat it. He also held the South African 100km record until Bongmusa Mthembu (also mentioned in this book) broke it in 2016. Bruce 's life has been dedicated to running and he has managed to give back to the sport by starting Park Run in South Africa with millions of members taking part all over the country. His book 'Winged Messenger' is a gem for any novice who is looking to run their first Comrades marathon.

1. What do you love about running and how did you get into it?

What I love about running now is that it is my special time; I need my run every day, either with friends or on my own. I can always miss a day; that is fine. I am not on a streak or anything. However, if I missed a second or third day, I would be a very grumpy person if I didn't have my run. That's what I love about it most. I enjoy racing when I can but if racing was to be taken away from me like it has done during Covid, then I am still enjoying my running. If I couldn't run, my family would have me put down. They know I would become very grumpy and unbearable to live with. I got into running at school. Whenever we had a sports day, most of my mates would be trying to get out of it and hide behind the cricket pavilion for a smoke and not run. I would say we have to do it. It's cross-country Wednesday afternoon lets go and run it. If it were the athletics, the teacher would say Fordyce, you are running the 1500 metres, I would say ok, I will run the 1500 metres. I gave up all sports when I first went to university and then I started running again, specifically to run the Comrades marathon. You must understand the Comrades marathon in South Africa is a bit like the FA Cup, Wimbledon and London marathon all rolled into one. It is a massive event in South Africa. The whole country watches it, and it is a huge event. Everybody knows about it and it is a great goal to go for and I started with the aim of running my first Comrades. My first Comrades, I ran just to finish, and I finished 43rd, which was still quite high in the field and I ran quite a good time. The second one I ran, I finished 14th and then my third Comrades, I placed 3rd. Once you have made the top three on the podium, you kind of think, I can win this. The following year I blew it and finished 2nd and the following year, I won it, so it took me five years to win it.

2. Have you ever had a 'did not finish' (DNF), if so, how did you react to it?

I have had quite a few DNF's in my life, funnily enough, not at Comrades. I have had some bad runs at Comrades, but Comrades has this atmosphere that even if you are having a bad day, you grab a beer from a spectator and you walk and finish because everybody respects you more. Obviously not if you are in danger with your health. I have had a DNF in a 10km race when I knew at 3km there was something wrong with me and I am not having a good run and I dropped out. I have never really had a problem with a DNF unless I couldn't explain why. Every time I have been able to explain why. Whether you are struggling with an injury or just not having a good day. It is something that is not frequent with me, but I have had the odd one. I haven't beaten myself up about it. If you are in the sport long enough, it is eventually going to happen. Also, if you are not a very good sporadic racer. I am very good at planning, plotting and peaking on the right day, or I was. In a sense, I made my own luck; I would go to the start line knowing I was going to have a good one because my training would tell me I was going to have a good one. I am not saying I knew I was going to win but I would know it was going to be a good day. Funnily enough, one race that comes to mind is a 100km race in Belgium in the summer and I was ready for it. My sister made the whole family a pasta dish two nights before, which I wolfed down and it had salmonella in it, so all of us were throwing up the whole night, it was not her fault because it was two nights before, I thought I would be ok on the day and on the day at about 50km, I realised I didn't feel good, and I dropped out of that one. That also didn't haunt me; it was the only ultra I think I ever dropped out of. It didn't haunt me because I knew the reason.

3. Who are your greatest inspirations and why (either in or out of the sport)?

Wow! Here in South Africa, Nelson Mandela, who I met on a couple of occasions when he was still alive. He was truly a great person. Running wise, it is all the heroes of the 60s and 70s who when I was starting out were my heroes. Ron Hill, who I have met a couple of times, Ron is a big hero. Billy Rodgers who won four Boston Marathons and four New York marathons. On the track Lasse Virén 'Flying Finn' who won four Olympic Gold medals at 5,000 and 10,000 metres. Kip Keino and I met him too and he was such a lovely guy. Because I sat spellbound and watched it, Neil Armstrong, landing on the moon was probably the most incredible thing I have ever seen in my whole life—witnessed. I was alive when England won the 1966 World Cup. I watched it in black and white as there was no colour televisions in those days. That was pretty amazing; Jeff Hurst hattrick, Bobby Moore, Bobby Charlton, just a great team.

4. Tell us about your greatest failure?

Probably not finishing my master's degree. I am an archaeologist, that's what I studied, and the archaeology of Africa is really where is it is all at. I was taught by some of the brightest people in that subject. I completed an honours degree and then I was doing my masters, then my running started to interfere. I started winning races even though it was at amateur level at the time; there was still prize money and TV endorsements and that kind of thing. I suddenly realised I could really do well at this, so I gave up my academic career and I never finished that degree. That's probably it. I remember my professor David Lewis Williams who is a genius in bushman rock art, said to me, 'Go Fordyce, fame and money appear to be your spurs.' He mocked me. My mother would say not winning ten Comrades because I have got one-second place. To this day, she has not forgiven me for not winning ten. I tell her, 'mum nine is not bad,' but she is still not happy. My family doesn't mind; my family thinks nine is great. Your mother is always your biggest critic, and that pushes you. She felt I should have won ten.

5. Tell us something interesting that not a lot of people know about you?

Probably that I am an archaeologist and a historian, they are my passions. A lot of people don't know that I was born in Hong Kong. My father was in the British army; he was a Gurkha. I lived in Hong Kong for a while.

6. How do you manage family or home life around running?

I manage the family and home life easily because it became a job. I can't think of a better job actually. I usually go running very early, I wake up very early and I am out the door. I like to have the day ahead of me. I don't win any races anymore but after running a race, the event organisers have me there to give the prizes out afterwards. In South Africa, my wife and I started park run. We started it in South Africa because park run in the UK was started by a South African, a good friend of ours called Paul Sinton-Hewitt. Paul is originally a Johannesburg boy. He emigrated to the UK and when I went over to run the London marathon, he asked me if I would start it in South Africa. At first, I was very sceptical but thank goodness we did. We are not as big as the UK, but it is still big. We are approaching 300 events and 1.2 million members. That takes up all my time now in a normal week. I love it. That's where I get a little competitive. I am in the 65-year-old category, so I can't win a park run anymore but if I see another balding grey-headed guy go shooting past me, I am off after him. Anyone in my age group, I hunt them down. My personal best for 5km in my career is 14:26 in a track race. My joy in that race was I just about avoided being lapped as the winner that day did it in about 13:26 or something like that. I think track sessions are very good for your ultra-running to work on your speed all the time because then your cruising speed improves. I think this is a badly neglected area of ultra-running. The best ultra-runners are fairly quick at shorter stuff. I always had this feeling that if I get towards the end of the race and I am shoulder to shoulder with another person that he better be a track runner because I know exactly what to do. I am going to push him in front of me and when there is 300 metres to go, I am going to take off. I kind of had that advantage over some of the pure ultra-guys that I had a bit of speed. Nothing that would scare anyone in Kenya but enough to get another ultra-runner to raise his eyebrows a little bit.

7. What are your interests outside running?

I really love going to the game reserves. They have magnificent elephants and rhino. We stay in a lovely chalet which has a watering hole just outside it. I am also keen on South African bird life. Kruger National Park is my idea of paradise. My children said to me that they will scatter my ashes on the Comrades marathon route. I said, why would you do that? That is the place I have experienced most pain and is the place I hated the most. I said, you must scatter my ashes on the edge of a stunning pond or dam in the Kruger National Park please. There are animals such as hippos and lions, that's where I am happiest. The only problem is you cannot go for a run there as you would get nailed. Now out of two weeks, I probably miss one day of running. Now I run more for pleasure, I meet up with people and run, maybe get a coffee and chat afterwards then on the weekend do a park run and go as hard as I can. When I miss a day, it is usually for work commitments, travel, and to be honest, a hangover. When we won the Rugby World Cup final, there was absolutely not a chance of going to go for a run the next day. We celebrated long, long into the night.

8. Do you have any race day rituals?

I wouldn't say I have rituals; I know some cricketers who have some rituals. I know a good friend who is a cricketer at the highest level, and he must make sure all the toilet seats in the changing room are down before going out to compete. Many athletes have their own sort of routines, such as Nadal, the tennis player. I don't really have any myself. I used to lay out all my gear on the floor in the order that I had to put it on, so I didn't miss something out. Socks, shoes etc.

I never eat before a marathon. My last meal would be the night before. I just have two cups of coffee for the caffeine and water. During the race, I might start taking in a gel or two. South African races start very early in the morning or at least 90% of them because of the heat.

Twitter @BruceFordycerun
Instagram @bruce_fordyce
www.brucefordyce.com

Michael Wardian

Michael enjoys competing in marathons and ultra-marathons. He has a long list of podium finishes throughout his running career. On top of his extensive list of podium finishes in both the marathon and ultra-marathon distances, he has set numerous world records. There are many to his name, including setting the fastest time for seven marathons on seven continents in seven days; talk about a productive week. He set the world record for the fastest time completing the 50km distance on a treadmill in a time of 2:59:49. He talks about how he likes to break a sweat daily, but I think these achievements are a little more than that. He set a world record in the Leadville 100 mile, one of the most renowned ultra-races in America. He has also completed some of the world's most punishing ultra-races on the planet, such as Bad-water Ultra-Marathon 135, Ultra Gobi 400km, and The UVU North Pole Marathon with temperatures dipping below negative 40 Celsius. There is plenty more than that as well. In 2017 Michael raced (not just ran) a staggering 1,610 miles. On top of all that, he has been named ultra-runner and master ultra-runner of the year several times.

1. What do you love about running and how did you get into it?

I love running because it is very precise and fair; if you do the work, you get the results. There is no hiding from running. Running will strip away all pretence and thoughts about who you think you are and reveal who you really are. I got into running to run the Boston Marathon once way back in 1993 and Boston was my first running goal. I didn't even know you had to qualify. I just wanted to run it after seeing my friend Vince Voisin's mom-Vickie's medal.

2. Have you ever had a 'did not finish' (DNF), if so, how did you react to it?

If you run long enough eventually, you will have a "DNF," and I have had a few. Most were not life-threatening but a few were pretty bad. What I learned is that most of the time, it takes longer to get back to your hotel or the start line than it does to just keep going.

3. Who are your greatest inspirations and why (either in or out of the sport)?

I am really inspired by driven people. It can be anyone who is dedicated to their craft and work religiously to improve themselves.

4. Tell us about your greatest failure?

The Barkley Marathons, I suck at that race still. I have had many failures but that has to be one of them, but you know the great thing, every failure has made me stronger and better.

5. Tell us something interesting that not a lot of people know about you?

I am pretty open with people. I guess something that people might not remember is that I played lacrosse growing up and was not a runner. I love to read and listen to podcasts & audiobooks at 2x speed so I can learn faster.

6. How do you manage family or home life around running?

I am really fortunate; our family is invested in me and my running, so getting my training in has always been straightforward, but I definitely try and be completely involved and engaged. So, for me, that means early mornings and using each moment.

7. What are your interests outside running?

I love running but I also enjoy other activities like Chess, Cycling, Foosball, Reading, Video Games, and coaching.

8. Do you have any race day rituals?

I like to break a sweat every day.

Instagram: @mikewardian
Twitter: @mikewardian
Facebook: www.facebook.com/michaelwardian
Website: www.mikewardian.com

Georgia Tindley

Georgia, who escaped the city life of London for the Highlands in Scotland, just loves to spend time moving her body out in nature. If she is not running, she will be either cycling, skiing, climbing, or walking. If you don't find her out and about, then she will be more than likely reading a book, one of her other passions in life. Her running career has seen her podium in all kinds of races, such as shorter brutal vertical climbs, marathons, and ultra-marathons. She also holds a couple of fastest known times (FKT) that were completed in 2020 in Scotland. She has competed in trail, sky, and mountain races representing Great Britain. In 2018 Georgia claimed 6th in the Tromsø Skyrace in Norway. The race itself is 57km with a 4,800-metre climb. In 2019 she won the Glen Coe Skyline race, which is a 52km race with an elevation of 4,750 metres.

1. What do you love about running and how did you get into it?

I love running because it is simple, because it is fun, because it gets me outside and gives me freedom. Whether I'm heading out on my local loop for the thousandth time or lacing up to explore somewhere new, the thrill is always there. I enjoy the movement of running—the ease of it, the fun, the rhythm, the adrenaline of crossing difficult terrain. I enjoy the places it takes me and the things I experience—distant mountains, meeting new friends, overcoming challenges, witnessing the changing seasons, competing across the world, interacting with wildlife.

2. Have you ever had a 'did not finish' (DNF), if so, how did you react to it?

Yes, I've had a few actually—from crumbling under the pressure at an English Schools XC when I was 12 (the first and last time my parents came to see me race) to being forced to drop out due to tendon injury at Sky Pirineu 2019. There have been times when I've pushed through a race when I probably shouldn't have; there have been times when I've dropped out when I probably shouldn't have. Running and racing, especially over ultra-distances, is about toeing a fine line between toughness and stupidity. More than anything, it is a learning process. Every DNF I've had, I've learnt something from. Sometimes it's about preparation, sometimes injury, sometimes mental strength. I don't think that a DNF is anything to be ashamed of—in many instances, it is the right decision to make, and in others, it will help you come back stronger next time.

3. Who are your greatest inspirations and why (either in or out of the sport)?

My greatest inspirations aren't runners but people who are bold enough to ignore the opinion of others and focus on what makes them tick. People throughout history who aren't afraid to live outside the norm, who embrace their individuality and carve their own path through life.

4. Tell us something interesting that not a lot of people know about you?

I love swimming but I'm really, really terrible at it. I can stay afloat, but not much more. No triathlons for me anytime soon.

5. How do you manage family or home life around running?

I often feel like I'm being pulled in many different directions all at once. I want to be good at my job and as a teacher of vulnerable children, I know that my work is important—sometimes I think I'm being selfish working part-time. I want to spend time with my family but know that I loathe London and can't spend more than a few days there. I love spending time with friends, but most of them don't want to go up a hill in the rain with me. I want to make myself a home in Scotland, but I also want to be able to travel and run all over the world. Everyone has multiple facets to their lives; we're all juggling different responsibilities and commitments. I know, however, that I wouldn't be a good teacher, daughter, sister, or friend if I wasn't doing the thing that I love most. Running is just a part of my life, but it underpins everything. That's why I prioritise it, and slowly my friends and family have come to understand that. Besides, as my brother will attest, if I've not been out running recently, I'm not much fun to be around!

6. What are your interests outside running?

I normally take any excuse I can to be moving and outside, so if I'm not running, you'll often find me cycling, skiing, climbing, or walking. If not, I'll have found a cosy corner to do some reading. I was brought up in a house full of books and have been reading for as long as I can remember. I read across most genres—crime, westerns, classics, poetry, autobiography, sport, education, travel, nature. I love that feeling of becoming totally absorbed in a book so that you unaware of your surroundings. As with running, it's the feeling of escape that I'm chasing.

7. Do you have any race day rituals?

Does running late and dashing for the start line count? I'm that girl who had to sprint back to the hotel because she forgot her number, arrives to register 10 minutes before the race starts, never has time for a warm-up, sneaks off for a last-minute wee, and has missed the start of a race on more than one occasion.

www.georgiatindley.com
Instagram @gtindley

Ian Sharman

an succeeds in running whether that is running races for himself or coaching runners. He is the Head Coach at Sharman Ultra, and they have a team of champion coaches comprising three of the top 10 ultra-runners of the decade according to Ultra Running Magazine. He has coached some of the world's elites notably Magda Boulet and Ellie Greenwood. His impressive running career has seen him complete over 200 ultra-races. Ian has won over 50 multi-day races/road marathons/trail ultras or adventure races with experience of running in many mountain ranges, including the Himalayas, Andes, Rockies and European Alps. He is the current record holder for the Grand Slam of ultra-running, which consists of a set of four of the five most respected and oldest 100-mile races in the United States. He has won Leadville 100 four times and is the only person in history to break 17 hours four times. Ian has far too many accolades to his name to mention them all. In addition to this Ian interestingly holds nine Guinness World Records for running marathons in costumes in the fastest times.

Anthony Rogan

1. What do you love about running and how did you get into it?

I saw a TV show about the Marathon des Sables through the Sahara Desert and decided I'd like to try it, so I started training at age 24. I've always loved travel and sport in general but I quickly got addicted to racing all over Europe and ran my first 100 marathons or ultras in a four-year period.

2. Have you ever had a 'did not finish' (DNF), if so, how did you react to it?

Yes, several DNFs. Usually, it's due to going into a race with some form of injury in the build-up, but sometimes purely due to not mentally preparing enough and therefore not having a strong reason why I cared about the race. That's such a key part to racing well and even just finishing really tough events, but it's easy to sign up for a race before working out what's important about the race and why I care enough to give it my best effort.

3. Who are your greatest inspirations and why (either in or out of the sport)?

I started racing when Haile Gebrselassie and Paula Radcliffe were at their peak, so I looked up to them and was lucky enough to race the Berlin Marathon one of the times Haile set the World Record. But otherwise, my main sporting heroes are from other sports, like Roger Federer in tennis, Lionel Messi and Ian Wright in football (I'm an Arsenal fan and Messi is just the GOAT).

4. Tell us about your greatest failure?

I'm constantly trying to improve and want to run faster times in my 40s than I did in my 30s (I was 30 seconds off my best marathon at the age of 40 a few months before writing this). But two things I really want to achieve that will make a perfect day are a win at the Western States 100 Miler in California, a gold medal (top 10) at Comrades in South Africa and a sub 2:30 flat marathon (I've run 2:21 downhill). If I never achieve them, then it's not like I feel like a failure, but they're three of my main motivators related to running.

5. Tell us something interesting that not a lot of people know about you?

I worked as an economist for almost a decade, including the first few years of racing, so that inspires the way I look at racing and problem-solving.

6. How do you manage family or home life around running?

Since 2011 I've been a full-time coach with complete control over my schedule, so that gives me a lot more flexibility to fit in running and other training (and means I don't have a commute). So, this isn't really an issue, despite being married since 2010…although it helps, we don't have kids.

7. What are your interests outside running?

I love reading, road-tripping and travel. Plus, I'm a video game geek and always like to have the latest console, spending a lot of time in the past year playing Zelda: Breath of the Wild.

8. Do you have any race day rituals?

I keep things as simple as possible around races since then; fewer things can go wrong. So, my only pre-race ritual for ultras is doing a few strides and warm-ups like I'd do before any race. I also aim to get into the moment before the starting gun and remind myself to enjoy it and that I'm there because it's an epic, beautiful challenge, not just a race.

Instagram and Twitter @sharmanian
www.sharmanultra.com

Ruth Croft

R uth has had numerous wins and podiums throughout her running profession. In the years 2017, 2018, and 2019 Ruth podiumed in nearly every race she entered. This includes winning the prestigious OCC at UTMB in 2018 and 2019. One of her most noteworthy wins is the 2nd place finish at the 2021 Western States 100. She is an ultra-runner who is clearly very versatile considering the results that she has claimed on the different types of courses. Not all ultra-runners can adjust to different courses, but the results show that this isn't a problem for Ruth. In addition to her huge success at UTMB and Western States 100, she has won Les Templiers, Marathon Ultra Pirineu and CR, and Giir Di Mont. She also got onto the podium with a second-place finish in the tough 120km Lavaredo Ultra. Recently, Ruth made history by setting a record on the 102km race at the 2021 Tarawera Ultramarathon. She set a record of 9:21:03 on the course, which was a new best for a female competitor. The New Zealander was the first female runner to gain the outright title in this race.

1. **What do you love about running and how did you get into it?**

I love its simplicity and discovering places with my own two feet. I love the physical benefits of running, but also the mental aspect of being able to constantly learn more about myself and push beyond my own perceived limits. Through trail running, you also meet some pretty rad people and go to some awesome places. In NZ, during primary school, it is compulsory to do cross country and athletics and so that was really my introduction into running. Also, my family used to go on multi-day tramps (Kiwi for hiking) and on the last day, I would always race against my dad, uncle, and brother. Although I always came last, it instilled a sense of competitiveness in me.

2. **Have you ever had a 'did not finish' (DNF), if so, how did you react to it?**

No, I have never had a DNF. People weigh a lot of importance on a DNF, but it is only what you make it out to be and it does not define you as a person or runner. What I believe is important is that you take what you learn from it, not dwell on it, and move forward. I imagine that mentally it can shake you and take some time to overcome but I also believe that if you prepare well for a race, then this significantly diminishes your chances of a DNF.

3. **Who are your greatest inspirations and why (either in or out of the sport)?**

Fellow kiwi Jonathon Wyatt has always been a great inspiration for me. Jono was World Mountain Running Champion six times but also represented NZ at the Olympics in the marathon. It is not very often that you meet a runner that can cross over disciplines and Jono was able to perform well on the road and in Mt running, which I find inspiring. His physical achievements aside, he is also very humble, down to earth which I am drawn to.

Another person who I have found inspiring lately is Dr. Stacy Sims, who has really brought to forefront the gender differences in exercise science and nutrition. Her famous tagline, "Women are not small men," is about how a lot of time training and nutrition advice is all taken from male studies and applied to females. This, therefore, does not take into account the female body and our continuous changing of hormones. Her work has really helped me in my own training and nutrition.

4. Tell us about your greatest failure?

I find within trail running that there is a lot of focus and hype on running 100miles. When I initially got into trail running, I started on this trajectory of wanting to run long—100km+ with ultimately Western States and UTMB in sight. My greatest failure was getting caught up in this hype and running longer ultras when I was not ready. I remember I had a really bad experience in a 120km ultra where I was throwing up and just not enjoying the whole experience. This race experience was a great wake-up call and it made me really question what I was doing and why I was doing it when I was not even having fun. After that, I dropped back down to shorter distances, worked on my speed and found the enjoyment again. I think it is important to make sure your intentions for racing are in the right place.

5. Tell us something interesting that not a lot of people know about you?

At the end of the year, for the past three years, I have dedicated 10 days for silent meditation. Over these 10 days, you are not allowed to read, write, speak, exercise, or use technology. It has become a really important time for me to step away from everything and work on my mind without the constant distractions that we have in everyday life.

6. How do you manage family or home life around running?

I have a partner, but we don't have kids, so for us as a couple, it is a lot easier to balance family and home life around running. Good organisation always helps and getting to bed early too!

7. What are your interests outside running?

I am currently studying Naturopathy. Alternative medicine and health and wellness is something I have always been passionate about. I also coach athletes online for any distance from shorter road races to trail ultras. Outside of running, I enjoy road biking, mountain biking, hiking, cold water therapy, and saunas.

8. Do you have any race day rituals?

Coffee with breakfast is as far as my race day rituals go.

Instagram @ruthcrofty
Facebook—Ruth Croft
Twitter @ruthcrofty

Sarah Moore

Ultra-races are what most people would call a crazy concept anyway, but Sarah has succeeded in arguably one of the most challenging ultras for the mind. The Ode to Laz Michigan Back Yard Ultra Sarah has won twice in 2019 and 2020. Not only did she win it, but her own performance increased dramatically as she ran an extra 12.5 miles in 2020 compared to her 2019 win. This is a race that requires runners to complete a 4.167-mile lap on the hour every hour and the winner is determined by the last person standing. If you are not ready to go again on the hour, then that's the end of the race. Sarah has also finished 3rd in numerous 100 milers, including Desert Solstice 100 miler, Canal Corridor 100-mile Endurance Run, and Brazos Bend 100 miler. Sarah is someone (like many) who after reading 'Born to Run,' was hooked on the ultra-scene. This is someone who is progressing every year in ultra-racing and it is exciting to see her development.

1. What do you love about running and how did you get into it?

I first looked at running as a way to stay fit for other sports during the off-season or as a punishment during practice. Then, after I stopped playing organized sports, it was a means to stay healthy and justify a few extra calories in the evening. But when I went through some life-changing events after college in my 20's, I learned it was about so much more than getting that calorie burn and runner's high. I found my adopted family in other runners. A support network of friends. And the act of running became an opportunity to share with them the highs and the lows of life. They were my therapists during dark times, propped me up, and got me through. And in the good times, they were my advocates and cheerleaders. I credit them for who I am. They saw potential in me that I could not see in myself. They inspired me to dream. And then to dream even bigger.

So, what do I love about running? Of course, I love the way it makes me feel, pushing my limits, exploring new places, being in nature, etc. But at the end of the day, it's really about the people for me. I love running because I love runners.

2. Have you ever had a 'did not finish' (DNF), if so, how did you react to it?

Yes. …Ouf! It still hurts. The sting of a DNF never leaves you. The Old Dominion 100 Miler in Virginia—June 2, 2018. I relive that night over and over in my head. I can still feel how raw and bloody my back was from the skin that had chaffed off due to my shorts & pack rubbing over the 22+ hours and 87.5 miles I had slogged, soaking wet. It was a mix of extreme heat and humidity during the day, followed by 8 hours of torrential rainfall through the night and I was a total novice at mountain races. I had a lot to learn about gear, staying dry, and mental toughness. Admittedly, I had gone into the race a little "cocky" with a goal to sub-24-hour Buckle or bust. And I busted. I had time to finish under the cut-off, but I was borderline hypothermic and wouldn't be able to get that "Buckle." So, with the buckle out of reach, miserable conditions, and unbearable pain, I rationalized quitting. But in hindsight, you always look back and say, dang. I could've/should've finished...

I did not finish, but I did not fail. It's only a failure if you don't learn something, and I learned some valuable lessons. I learned about suffering. I learned about carrying your rain jacket with you, ALWAYS! I learned about humility and level setting expectations. I learned you should never underestimate how hard a 100-mile race is going to be and to go into it with a few goals in mind because it won't always go to plan, and that's ok. Just switch to plan B. or C. The worst part about that DNF is that part of the reason I "quit" was because I wouldn't buckle. But at the post-race breakfast, as I sulked and picked at my eggs, I learned that all finishers receive a finishers gift, and this year was a race pint glass. And I LOVE PINT GLASSES!!!! I was so mad at myself for not crawling the remaining 13 miles to the finish line for that alone and became determined to come back and finish no matter what. And so, the next year, I did. Didn't "buckle," but it didn't matter. I PR'd and treasure to this day my Old Dominion finisher's dry bag... even though it's not a pint glass. (Apparently, the pint glasses were a one-time thing).

3. Who are your greatest inspirations and why (either in or out of the sport)?

I credit my friend, Mike Fisher, for inspiring me to attempt my first ultras. He lent me his copy of "Born to Run" and after reading that, I was hooked on going the distance. As I've progressed, I have looked up to other big names like Courtney Dauwalter and Maggie Guterl, who have impressive ultra-running accomplishments under their belts. "Empowered females, empower females," and they made me realize that if they can do it, why can't I? More recently, I have been inspired by the Barkley Marathons and other Lazarus Lake "challenges." At first, I dreamed of running Barkley. But as I learned more about it and got to know an original "Barker," Mike Dobies (a native Michigander, who I also admire and look up to for inspiration), I realized I was not cut out for it. ...Yet... I guess it's still a dream, but one I am working toward and realize I am a loooong way off.

4. Tell us about your greatest failure?

I've definitely let myself down a few times, but I'm not sure I look back on those occasions as failures. Even the DNF at Old Dominion wasn't a total failure because it became my fuel in future races and provided perspective on what is "hard." I guess if I am honest, the biggest "failure" that I can think of recently was not giving everything I had in Bigs Backyard last year. I should've gone one more. After 200 miles, I wasn't done-done. I didn't "time out" like I had promised myself I would. I slow-rolled the last yard so that my crew would not have time to talk me into going out for another. I was scared that if I did, I would realize I *could* finish another, and it would never end. I mentally failed myself when the physical was still "OK." I know it is always easy to say after the fact, but I will always look back and wonder, what if I hadn't sandbagged the last one and gone back out for one more?

5. Tell us something interesting that not a lot of people know about you?

I grew up on the chubby side until I hit my growth spurt in high school. Being a lover of food and overweight, I struggled with body issues. I definitely was not the fast kid in gym class or in team sports. I had to work at it. I remember my mom telling me that if I wanted to lose weight, I should try walking around the block and work up to running, but I was too lazy back then. I never dreamed I would become a runner. I never aspired to be fast. I always had this negative association with running and didn't realize it could be "fun" until I met my running family as an adult. And when I started running trails with them, I initially HATED the trails. They were SO hard. It took a few years and many injuries to get my "trail-sense" and embrace trail running. Then, I realized it was something I loved. And then I started to "compete." Looking back now, it's crazy to see how far I've come and what is possible if you just get out there and do it.

6. How do you manage family or home life around running?

Luckily, my husband and I got into distance running together and it is something we share. When it comes to logging big mileage weeks leading up to a race, he's usually doing it with me. Even if he's not signed up for a particular race, he supports and crews me. I used to drag my step kids out for local races when they were younger or force them to ride their bikes while we ran long, but now that they are older, they have other hobbies and things they would rather be doing, so I don't force them to join as much. Other than that, running is my "home life." It's a lifestyle. It is as necessary as breathing. We don't look at it like something we have to try and fit into our schedule, but rather it takes priority, and other things fit in around it.

7. What are your interests outside running?

I love travelling and being outside. I love playing sports, strategy board games, and card games. I enjoy puzzles and crosswords. I taught myself the piano when I was younger with just 1 year of rudimentary lessons. I'm not great, but I like to teach myself new songs now and then. I love a challenge or an adventure and seizing the moment. I like telling jokes and hearing jokes and being goofy, in general. I love talking about running.

8. Do you have any race day rituals?

Not really. I usually treat race day like any other long-run day to stay relaxed and calm. The greatest part about ultra-racing is that it lasts so long, so you don't really have to stress about things like you might going into a shorter distance. You accept things like the fact that you'll probably have to poo at some point during, so it doesn't matter if you go beforehand. You can settle in for the long-haul and take whatever comes in stride. Ann Trason describes it perfectly in Born to Run; it's "like easing your body into a hot bath."

Instagram and Twitter @smooremiles
www.mooremiles.com

John Fegyveresi

J ohn has been in the ultra-game long enough that looking over his racing CV, there are not many races that he hasn't completed in the US. He holds the title for being the slowest finisher in the Barkley Marathons with a time of 59:41:21 (the cut off is 60 hours). This is not to say that he hasn't won some of the shorter distances in ultra-running. But it does seem that John succeeds in the races that seem to really test the mind on the longer distances. He has completed and podiumed at some of the most brutal mind-pounding races on the planet. Those that know about Barkley Marathons will know that completing the race within the cut-off point is an achievement very few competitors have earned. A lot of runners would not even comprehend taking on the mammoth task of the race. Put it this way, in this unique race, if you complete 60 miles of the 100-mile course, it is considered a 'fun run' and most that attempt the Barkley Marathons are elated with getting to the 60-mile point. As mentioned already, John has an impressive running CV; amongst his CV are completions of some of the most legendary US ultra-races, including Badwater 135, Leadville Trail 100 miler, HURT 100, and Miwok 100km. In addition to this, he has finished 2nd on two occasions Vol State 500km unaided. Interestingly, John is an Assistant Professor of Practice, School of Earth and Sustainability at Northern Arizona University.

1. What do you love about running and how did you get into it?

Mostly just that it allows me to explore…if that makes sense. My favourite running outings are the ones where I am not necessarily training or have any sort of set goal…but rather, I'm just out playing in the woods on beautiful and twisty trails. When I am training for something bigger, I don't always enjoy those daily runs, but I suppose I do enjoy the knowledge that I'm working towards something bigger, and that is a pretty rewarding feeling. Knowing that just through repetition, discipline, and a healthy lifestyle, I can realize those cumulative efforts at a capstone race or event. It is definitely a great feeling finishing a race that you've worked so hard to train for. As far as actual races, events, and adventures….I suppose my favourites, are the ones that are more non-traditional and more like adventures than just typical races. So…my AT and PCT thru-hikes, my hiking around the backcountry of New Zealand, the Barkley Marathons, Vol State, Hardrock, Long-Trail FKT Attempts, and any race or event that is really low-key, no-frills, and really takes the runners out to the middle of no-where.

2. Have you ever had a 'did not finish' (DNF), if so, how did you react to it?

Sort of. I have never DNF'd any sort of traditional race or event…but I have quit early several times at the Barkley Marathons (which I sort of put in its own category). While I did finish Barkley in 2012, during each of my subsequent 3 runnings, I failed to make all 5 loops ever again.

3. Who are your greatest inspirations and why (either in or out of the sport)?

I suppose I have many. In running/adventuring, I can certainly think of a few names: Blake Wood, Travis Wildeboer, Maggie Guterl, Jennifer Pharr Davis, but I think there are so many out there that maybe aren't quite as known that, through their running, are inspiring so many others out there (perhaps without even knowing just how much). People like Mirna Valerio or Randy Pierce. I think maybe it's those folks at your work or in your neighbourhood that you see out every day at 6 am logging miles, who are the ones that perhaps have the greatest impact on others, without even knowing it. Outside of running, there are certainly countless others who have inspired me through the years, many of which are somewhat cliché (father, mother, spouse, good friend, etc). Personally, I think those out there that have had either a strong connection to nature or a strong drive for exploration are those that speak to me the loudest. Those like John Muir, Ernest Shackleton, Nimblewill Nomad, the countless long-distance thru-hikers, world travellers, motorcycle adventurers etc. and of course, last but not least, all of those lucky enough to have been selected as astronauts.

4. Tell us about your greatest failure?

I've certainly had my share of failures throughout my life…some personal, some professional, some with my adventures, but it's hard for me to state emphatically my "greatest." I think all of my failures have helped to mould me into who I am today and have played a large part in how I've grown and matured as a person and adventurer.

If I were to frame my failures in such a way to ask myself, "Which of my failures has had the greatest impact or influence on the trajectory of my life?"...I suppose I would say either my failure to have had more consistent relationship with my dad before he passed or maybe my failures related to my first long-term relationship. In the running world, the failure that had the greatest effect on me was the monumental failure I experienced in my 2nd year (2013) at the Barkley Marathons (after having finished the year prior). That really messed me up for a while. Thankfully, I learned from it and came back in 2014 to redeem myself with a 3-loop fun run. Lastly, I guess professionally, what seems like the biggest failure to me, is that I never made it through the astronaut candidate selection program. I have tried for over 20 years to be selected. Regardless of my personal growth and never-ending drive to keep learning and become more qualified, in each of the 5 calls I've applied to, I've failed to even make the final interview stage.

5. Tell us something interesting that not a lot of people know about you?

I suppose I would start by quoting Melville in Moby Dick, "As for me, I am tormented with an everlasting itch for things remote." What I mean to say is that for as long as I can remember, I've wanted to find and experience the most remote places. I have wanted to find that patch of land in the woods that was the farthest from anyone else. It's kind of a weird sentiment, but I think there have been many others in history with a similar "itch."

As far as a fun anecdote that people might not know is that I was technically the first person to reach the South

Pole in 2016. I was deployed to the South Pole in late 2015 as part of an ice-core research project, and on the evening of Dec 31st, I walked out to the official marker just before local midnight so that I would be the first person "at the south pole" in 2016. I laughed about it, took a few pictures, and then went back inside to warm up. Something else many don't know about me was that for most of my time in middle school, I was certain I wanted to be an entomologist. I collected insects and even researched what colleges I wanted to attend. It was only after high school that my interests changed. Lastly, one running-related story.... during my very first race in 7th grade cross-country, I came in absolute dead last place. I was wearing a torn t-shirt and sweatpants, and horrible shoes. I didn't want to be there, but I told my dad I'd try it. By the end of that year, I ran a 5-minute mile and was among the top 5 on the team. In addition, my lifelong love of exploration and moving by foot really grew from that experience.

6. How do you manage family or home life around running?

I sort of just try to let it flow with however my life situation is. Sometimes, I have a lot of things due for work, or am prepping a lot of material for classes and need to ease back the running some. Other times, I'm in a lull or have more free time and pick it up more. But…running is also a way for me to clear my head and de-stress, so when I'm most stressed, I find going for a run (even if I don't necessarily have a lot of time for it) really helps ease any anxiety. Every time I've left on a run feeling anxious and stressed, I always come back feeling centred and calm. Often, whatever things I'm trying to sort out, I can do on a run. I probably sorted out more than half of the major questions and roadblocks with my dissertation while running.

7. What are your interests outside running?

I have a lot of "exploration" and "outdoor"-related interests. My true passion for motion is long-distance hiking. I've through-hiked many trails and still come back to that as my favourite mode of travel. I also like exploring by bike (road and mountain). I used to enjoy these types of activities the most on my own and in very large doses...but now I find I truly enjoy most of these types of activities in smaller doses and with my partner. I have evolved quite a bit in that sense...and really for the better. I still like my solo adventures from time-to-time, but there is just something special about sharing your explorations with someone else. More recently, I have been doing a lot of exploration on my small dual-sport adventure motorcycle and am already planning many camping, hiking, riding trips for next summer.

8. Do you have any race day rituals?

Nothing really special or different, I suppose. Some stretching, a lot of pre-race hydration, and just trying to calm my heart rate with deep breaths. I guess I do lay out my gear somewhat ahead of time to make sure I don't forget anything, but nothing crazy OCD or anything. When I'm at a start line, I try to "slow down the moment" and just absorb everything my senses will allow me to. I try to capture the feelings and images as best I can and always tell myself to savour the experience and exploration that is about to begin. After an event....well, I guess I would say there is almost always ice cream involved.

Twitter and Instagram @lakewoodhiker
http://lakewoodhiker.blogspot.com/
http://youtube.com/on2feet
Research site—http://johnfegy.weebly.com/

Tyler Green

Tyler has had many notable running performances and despite being a sponsored athlete running is not his main 'hustle' as he calls it. His daytime job is teaching and inspiring middle school students at a small private school. He also coaches high school track and cross country. I think it is fair to say that the students are in safe hands with Tyler's running credentials. He clearly has a passion for travel and adventure; he spent time living in Libya and Nepal. Tyler has won numerous races and placed top three in several others, but he has also had success in breaking several FKTs. As Tyler puts it 'FKTs are a little different to races as there is no podium finish,' it is either you beat the FKT, or you don't. It couldn't be any simpler. In 2020 Tyler set the FKT for the Wonderland Trail and Loowit Trail and in 2018, he set the FKT for Timberline Trail and Snoqualmie Pass to Stevens Pass. In competitive races, his most impressive result is the 2nd place finish in 2021 Westerns States 100. Some of his other significant performances are 1st place finishes in Black Canyon 100k, Bandera 100k, and Cascade Crest 100.

1. What do you love about running and how did you get into it?

I've been running from a very young age and always enjoyed the challenge of endurance sports. I love the process of training and seeing the incremental progress that consistent practice brings. I find running deeply meditative whenever I'm out on the roads or trails like my body and mind are fully one. That happens wherever I run, but of course, the primary joy I find in running is when I'm exploring beautiful places.

2. Have you ever had a 'did not finish' (DNF), if so, how did you react to it?

I recently DNF'd a race due to an ankle sprain. It was already a pretty miserable day with horrible weather, and I had entered the race on a whim. That said, it didn't affect me too much, but I was still disappointed not to finish.

3. Who are your greatest inspirations and why (either in or out of the sport)?

It's been incredible to watch Kipchoge as an example of excellence and the path to near perfection. He demonstrates the importance of community, mental strength, and day-in day-out training. That's pretty inspirational. I also really like to watch Des Linden as someone who "keeps showing up." I'm not the most talented runner but I've gained a lot of confidence by simply watching her progress through consistent, no-frills training.

4. Tell us about your greatest failure?

I mean, I don't count anything as a huge failure. I trained too hard when I first started ultrarunning, leading to a stress fracture, but that led to important lessons about how much volume my body could handle and taking a more measured approach. There's a lesson to be found in every race. The one that does sting is taking a wrong turn with 3k to go at Lavaredo. I'd fought really hard for a top-10 finish and lost 4 places due to the mistake.

5. Tell us something interesting that not a lot of people know about you?

I lived in Nepal for two years, working for an international development organization. I didn't even think about trail running and I'm so bummed I didn't find the sport sooner. This was in 2004. But I did hike, and I think some of my strengths as a runner came from this time of hiking up and down steep mountains in the Himalayas. They don't make switchbacks there.

6. How do you manage family or home life around running?

My wife and I are both runners and we don't have kids, so we can pretty much run to our hearts' content. We connect well when we're on weekend adventures together, driving and sleeping in our 1991 Toyota Previa van. That said, there are certain weeks that are busier than others. When I notice these kinds of weeks approaching, I usually dial back training and focus on work and count the week as mostly for recovery. That helps avoid burnout and I'm ready to go again when I can train hard when work allows.

7. What are your interests outside running?

I read a lot and enjoy thinking about the philosophy of story and storytelling. My wife and I like being outside a lot, so we ski and bike as well.

8. Do you have any race day rituals?

I used to think that race day rituals would make or break a race, but as I've progressed, my biggest race morning ritual is to stay really relaxed and don't let anything get to me. Just get ready to get down to business. Honestly, if there's one thing I really need before a race, it's some coffee and a good bowel movement. It'll be a good day if I get that done. The day before a big race, I was trying to figure out the optimal time to do my pre-race shakeout. My buddy said, "don't overthink it," and that's really good advice for all aspects of race preparation.

Instagram @narrowgreenarrow
www.ultrasidehustle.com

FOOD FOR THOUGHT

I think we can all agree that any ultra- events of any sort are brutal. If running ultra-distances of 50km and over aren't bad enough to push you mentally and physically, the last thing you need is another problem to have to worry about during an event. When most people prepare for a race, they probably have the usual thoughts, 'Am I fit enough?' 'Can I finish?' 'Have I forgotten any of my race gear?' Not many people apart from experienced / elite runners would have even considered worrying about gut issues ruining their chances of success on the course. Interestingly studies have shown that this is a common reason that ultra-runners DNF or under-perform in a race. Everyone talks a lot about how fit they feel from the training they have done but I cannot imagine that many people talk about or even practice training their gut. Stuempfle and Hoffman (3) carried out a study during the Western States Endurance Run to determine the incidence, severity, and timing of gastrointestinal (GI) symptoms in finishers and non-finishers. The results showed that among race finishers, 43.9% reported that GI symptoms affected their race performance, with nausea being the most common symptom (86%). Among race non-finishers, 35.6% reported that GI symptoms were a reason for dropping out of the race, with nausea being the most common symptom (90.5%). Stuempfle and Hoffman conclude that GI symptoms are very common during ultra-marathon running. So, what can be done to avoid this issue when out on the course? Obviously, no two people are the same, so the most important aspect as an ultra-runner is to experiment during training with the things that do or don't upset your gut. You know your body better than anyone else, no matter what research is done. Having said that, Parnell (4) and her research team have done some fascinating research into what food choices pre-exercise runners restricted to avoid gastrointestinal symptoms. The results were interesting. You might be delighted to find that this study helps solve some gut issues that affect your own performance or be devasted as it could ruin you enjoying your favourite foods free of guilt before the race. I apologise in advance. It was concluded that runners regularly avoided meat (32%), milk products (31%), fish/seafood (28%), poultry (24%), and high-fibre foods (23%). Caffeinated beverages were commonly avoided in events 10 km or less. I think I can speak for most ultra-runners and state that you will be risking yourself harm if you try to take away my pre-race coffee, no matter what studies show. Although it is great that there are studies that are available and we can learn from these to adapt points into our own pre-race eating habits, I still think there is a strong argument that the number one thing you can do is to experiment on yourself. Studies are a great tool for ideas of what may or may not work, but surely the key is to try the food out in your own training and see what works best for you. In addition to this, in a podcast with Registered Dietician Patrick Wilson and one of the foremost experts on athlete gut disorder with Training Peaks (5), Patrick discusses current studies looking into the potential benefits of practicing mindfulness to relieve gut problems before a race. At the time of writing, much of the research is still in the experimental stage; however, it may be something that a runner wants to experiment with themselves to relieve pre-race anxiety. After all any potential benefits come at no cost and no drawbacks.

John Kelly

onsidering that John, as of 2013, had never raced more than 10km it is quite astonishing what he has achieved in ultra-running. He was the 15th person to complete the Barkley Marathons in 2017, a race we know as being one of the toughest races on the earth. Some would argue that it is the toughest one around. Since starting in 1986, The Barkley Marathons is a race like no other, with close to a 100% failure rate. If you just stop and think about that, you'll realise how much of an achievement completing this immense race is; John was the 15th person to complete the race that started in 1986. On the 16th July 2020, John set the fastest known time on the Pennine Way (268 miles), which had not been broken in 31 years with a time of 2 days 16 hours and 46 minutes. This record was then broken by Damian Hall (also featured in the book) eight days later. John reclaimed this back in 2021 with a time of 2 days 10 hours 4 minutes and 53 seconds. If taking on and breaking the FKT on the Pennie Way was not enough, John several weeks later took on what he termed the 'Grand Round' in the UK. This challenge consists of completing the UKs big three rounds, which are challenges that many ultra-runners take on individually and try to complete in under 24 hours.

Anthony Rogan

John also cycled the distances in between each one. The challenges are in Wales, England (Lake District), and Scotland. This had never been completed before. The big three rounds had been completed together before but never with someone cycling in between each one. John on August 21, 2020, pulled off the incredible achievement in a total time of 130 hours, 43 minutes and 10 seconds. He ran two of the three rounds in under 24 hours. The whole challenge included a total of 185 miles of running with 25,440m of elevation gain over 113 summits, plus more than 400 miles of biking. It will be exciting to see how the 'Grand Round' develops amongst the running community.

1. What do you love about running and how did you get into it?

I've been running as long as I can remember, chasing my older brother and cousins around the farm where I grew up in the Tennessee mountains. In a way, it's something that takes me back to that childhood sense of freedom, temporarily disconnecting and recharging from day-to-day stresses. I also love the sense of exploration, which is one reason I particularly love trail running.

2. Have you ever had a 'did not finish' (DNF), if so, how did you react to it?

I've had a number of DNFs, but most not in the traditional sense. I've DNF'd at the Barkley Marathons 3 times on top of my 1 finish, and the first time I attempted it, I DNF'd one of my big personal challenges (The Grand Round, which links the UK's big 3 fell running rounds by bike). I look at these as the result of proper goal setting. Of course, I never want to fail, and I'm disappointed immediately following, but if I never come up short, then I'm not trying to reach far enough. Those failures resulted in some of my greatest improvements both as a runner and a person and propelled me to greater future success.

3. Who are your greatest inspirations and why (either in or out of the sport)?

As an adult, I've never wanted to look to specific people for inspiration. Many people, sometimes the most unexpected and overlooked, do inspiring things. And at some point everyone, even the most highly regarded, comes up short and lets others down. I prefer to focus on actions for inspiration. That might include the person(s) behind the action and their background story and circumstances, but it can come from anywhere—from running to those addressing major social issues to random acts of kindness from complete strangers.

4. Tell us about your greatest failure?

My one DNF in a "normal" race was at Ronda dels Cims in 2019. Unlike other DNFs I would legitimately classify it as a failure because it was due to improper preparation and I wasn't able to learn or grow much from it. Those things will inevitably happen, though, if we're challenging ourselves and putting ourselves out there. The best thing I can take away from it is to not repeat the same mistake. To rub salt in the wound, the race has now been permanently cancelled, so I'll be unable to give it another go.

5. Tell us something interesting that not a lot of people know about you?

I don't get brain freezes. It's my superpower. I can take the biggest slushie or milk-shake that exists and eat it as fast as possible, and I'm fine. That power is kind of cancelled out by the fact that I can't whistle; at all.

6. How do you manage family or home life around running?

Before Covid cancelled commutes, all of my weekday's miles were from my commute—running to and from the office. That was huge for me. Now I work my runs around family and work schedules and run my oldest son to school (he rides his bike). In the end, it's all about communication, compromise, and being sure everyone's on the same page as far as plans and expectations go. I also don't really do an enormous amount of training relative to what might be expected for the races I do. My weekly hours are on par with most serious marathon runners.

7. What are your interests outside running?

I'm a leader at a startup and have 4 young kids. I really don't have time for interests outside of running, and I don't say that jokingly. Some people might grimace at that, but it's the life I chose, and I love it. Once upon a time, I was a pretty serious water skier, World of Warcraft player, and fan of team sports.

8. Do you have any race day rituals?

I used to, but at some point, I realized that they mostly just add stress and the potential for something else to go wrong (e.g. one of the rituals not happening just right). One of my best races ever was where I got a stomach bug from my kids the night before and had absolutely none of my usual evening or morning prep. It forced me to focus on the race and the things I could actually control.

Instagram and Facebook @Randomforestrunner
www.randomforestrunner.com

Michael McKnight

As if ultra-distances like 100km or 100 miles aren't sufficiently amazing feats of endurance already, athletes like Michael really make you wonder what the human body and mind is really capable of. Michael has had success at the 100 miles and under ultra-distances, but he has really thrived when the miles are pushed far beyond 100 miles. In 2017 and 2019, he was the winner of the 'Triple Crown of 200s—200 Miler Slam'. Winning this title means having success in three races combined with being crowned Triple Crown champion. The three ultra-races are Moab 240 Endurance Run, Tahoe 200 Endurance Run, and Bigfoot 200 Endurance Run. Yes, that means that all three of the races are 200 miles and more, with Moab 240 being a 238 miler. In his 2017 win, he placed 3rd, 4th, and 7th and this was enough for him to win the overall Triple Crown. In 2019 he went one better, winning the event outright by finishing 1st in all three of the ultras. This means that Michael was running for a total of 162 hours and 51 seconds which was a new overall course record. To top it all off, these ultras are all scheduled only two months apart. The determination and discipline to run these kinds of races is only admirable. In addition to this, he also set the FKT in September 2020 for the Colorado Trail, 500 miles that run from Denver to Durango.

1. What do you love about running and how did you get into it?

I love the self-fulfilment feeling you receive from running. Being able to push your limits both physically and mentally is addicting for me. Being able to do something that you once thought impossible is so gratifying. I got into it due to my sister challenging me to do a half marathon with her. I had nothing better to do, so I signed up and went for it. The race experience was good enough for me to keep doing it.

2. Have you ever had a 'did not finish' (DNF), if so, how did you react to it?

In my ultra-running career, I've had one DNF. It was in 2014 at the Zion 100k. I felt awful for quitting. I actually went back to the aid station captain a few minutes later and asked to continue. But he informed me that my name was pulled, and I couldn't get back in. It was a bad enough experience that I've made sure to never quit a race since.

3. Who are your greatest inspirations and why (either in or out of the sport)?

My wife. She is so selfless and helps me in so many ways. From crewing me at a 200-mile race while also taking care of our new-born son to letting me go running every morning without complaint. She's so supportive. Also, Jeff Browning and Zach Bitter. They inspired me to take a new, less accepted path to nutrition with ultra-running. They coached me through the adaptation phase, and still continue to coach me on it. I'm so thankful for their help as well as their dedication to the sport.

4. Tell us about your greatest failure?

All through high school, I didn't try hard enough to be great. I was afraid of getting tackled in football. I didn't want to train to improve my skills. I told myself that I was an overweight farmer that didn't have any athletic talents. Not trying hard enough is my biggest failure to date.

5. Tell us something interesting that not a lot of people know about you?

I used to be a Country Swing Dance instructor.

6. How do you manage family or home life around running?

I get up early before my family wakes up. Most days I'm done with my running and strength training by the time they are up and ready for the day.

7. What are your interests outside running?

I'm an advocate for Down syndrome adoption. I love country swing dancing. Big into board games and video games. Love backcountry skiing.

8. Do you have any race day rituals?

Wake up early enough to poop two or three times before the race starts.

Instagram @thelowcarbrunner
www.lowcarb-runner.com

Ricky Lightfoot

At the age of fourteen, Ricky was introduced to fell running by the caretaker at his school. Even though in his first fell race he got lost on the course it did not put him off continuing with running. Years on his running has seen him win races in fell, trail, and ultra-distances. He has won numerous of the most notable fell races, including the Three Peaks Race, Wasdale, Borrowdale, Ennerdale, and Skiddaw. Ricky won the first ultra-marathon he entered in 2012, the Hammer Trail in Denmark. In 2015 he won the Ultra Skymarathon Madeira. He has represented Great Britain numerous times and ran races all over the globe, winning numerous of them along the way. He now lives in the Lake District in the UK, where he gets to enjoy the fells and stunning views on a daily basis. Ricky also works as a firefighter. And to think, the caretaker at my school didn't even change the toilet roll regularly.

1. What do you love about running and how did you get into it?

I love to explore, and I love to keep fit by running, especially on the fells of the Lake District; it allows me to do both almost every day. I also compete but if someone told me I could never race again, I don't think it would bother me, as long as I can run. Over the years, I know my running has developed into an obsession. I got into running by chance really; at secondary school, the caretaker came around our year group to ask if anyone would like to try a fell race, so I jumped at the chance. I along with a few mates, turned up on a typical West Cumbrian winters day in January, it was raining, cold and the trails were running like rivers. I started the under 16's race along with others and ended up getting lost, spending another 20 or so minutes out there running than I should have been. When I eventually made it to the finish, I was covered in mud, sheep shit and soaked to the skin. From then on, I was hooked.

2. Have you ever had a 'did not finish' (DNF), if so, how did you react to it?

Throughout the 20 years I've been running, I've only ever had to retire from a race twice; both of those times, the race was The Yorkshire 3 Peaks and both times through injury. Both times when I started, I knew that a DNF could be a likely outcome, so on both occasions, it didn't bother me so much, but injuries are never easy and the latter of those DNF's at the 3 Peaks was a big injury that required an operation and 18 months of rehab. A lot goes through your head during those times, highs, lows, persistently asking myself if I could actually get back to the level I was at and it was actually worth it? I'm not a professional or even making a living from it, at the end of the day it's a hobby.

3. Who are your greatest inspirations and why (either in or out of the sport)?

I've always admired those that are out double the winners time; those that are running near the back of the "pack" are giving and working just as hard as the leaders, they need to carry more water, food and possibly more kit to get them through, without these people, racing wouldn't be the same.

4. Tell us about your greatest failure?

This is a tough one, I've had failures but none I believe to be significant. I'll give this one a think and get back to you... (I am still waiting Ricky).

5. Tell us something interesting that not a lot of people know about you?

I once rescued a lamb on Great Gable and I recorded it on my camera; it later went viral and at last count, had 23 million views.

6. How do you manage family or home life around running?

Managing family, work and training is sometimes difficult; I think it helps to have a flexible approach to training. I don't set any times or arrange to meet people as sometimes I don't know if I'll get out running at 1000hrs in the morning or 1000hrs at night; I do have in my head what I want to do that day/week but it's always subject to change. What does help is that I have an understanding and supportive partner who sees that I'm obsessed, I have a job which I work shifts of 2 days, 2 nights, and 4 days off, this allows me to train in the daylight most days and I also get to use the gym and treadmill at work. My daughter has shown interest in running of late and we sometimes go out together, we don't go far but we're outside and she loves exploring the small trails from home in whatever the weather.

7. What are your interests outside running?

I love spending time with the family, we've just added a new addition to the family, a little boy, brother to his older sister Isobelle. I've tried lots over the years; I enjoy going to the gym, cycling, swimming, and more recently open water swimming in the Lake. It gives me a real adrenaline rush; swimming with only shorts on in winter is an amazing experience.

8. Do you have any race day rituals?

I don't have any race day rituals for a while though I did turn up to races late, giving myself only minutes to catch the start line. The last race I went to do in February 2020 I missed all together.

Instagram and Twitter @rickylightfoot

David Laney

D avid has been running most of his life; by the time he was six or seven, he was running nearly every day of the week. During his school and college life, he was running mostly track, with a couple of half-marathons also thrown into the mix. It wasn't until 2012 that David's passion for mountain and trail running really began. It was 2012 when he met Erik Skaggs, former Waldo 100Km course-record holder, and Hal Koerner, two-time Western States winner, who introduced him to running mountains. Since then, his running has gone from strength to strength, including some impressive wins and podiums on some of the toughest races in the world. One of his most notable performances is his 3rd place finish in the notorious 105-mile UTMB held in Chamonix in the French Alps. Not many American ultra-runners can say that they have podiumed on arguably the hardest ultra in Europe. In 2016 he got close to repeating his amazing success by achieving a 4th place finish. 2015 was a huge year for David as it also saw him earn the title Ultra-runner of the year, which meant that he was the youngest ever to achieve this acclaimed title. He has many other impressive podium finishes ranging in ultra-distances, including the winner of Rocky Racoon 100 miler,

3rd place North Face Endurance Challenge, and winner of Bandera 100k to name a few. One of his dreams from his childhood was to run and win the Western States 100. His best result to date is the 8th place finish in his wonder year of 2015; it will be exciting to see if David ever reaches his goal to win this race because he certainly has the ability.

1. **What do you love about running and how did you get into it?**

I started running with my dad when I was about 4 years old. I really enjoyed it from a young age and then went on to run cross country and track in the city league in elementary and middle school. I was lucky to have amazing coaches and mentors during my high school and college years and am thankful to have people who helped me along the way.

2. **Have you ever had a 'did not finish' (DNF), if so, how did you react to it?**

I have DNF'd once due to a twisted ankle. It was a bummer but not a big deal. I just learned that I needed a better headlight to illuminate the trail in the dark and that I needed to do more ankle strengthening exercises.

3. **Who are your greatest inspirations and why (either in or out of the sport)?**

Ernest Shackleton is a great explorer. I also like C. S. Lewis writings, and mostly my teammates inspire me.

4. **Tell us about your greatest failure?**

Biggest failure is probably putting running in front of other things in my life. I believe running is a great joy but is not the end of the world, and I made it the top priority for many years, which was an unfortunate mistake.

5. **How do you manage family or home life around running?**

Yes, waking up early is the only way to do it. I get up very early, make the coffee, feed the dog, do morning reading and prayers and then get out on the trails before the day really gets going. If running is a priority, and you have family, work, life stuff, you have to get up early or stay out late, or else things can get in the way.

6. What are your interests outside running?

I enjoy water colouring, hiking, being in the mountains, reading, and hanging out with my dog!

7. Do you have any race day rituals?

I wake up early, eat a bit of food with tea, and do my best to get to the starting line with time to use the porta-bathroom before the line gets too long.

Instagram @davidlaney12
www.trailsandtarmac.com

Martin Kern

There are many top ultra-runners who have inspiring stories about how they got into the sport. Martin is one of them. After recognising that he had lost his way a little, he took a career break in 2016 from his desk job so he could rebalance his life again. He certainly achieved this as numerous years on, he is hooked to running in the mountains. He loves running in the mountains that much he decided after a couple of successes in ultra-races to move to Vallouise in France, where he does most of his training. Martins ultra-journey started after he was living in New Zealand and he signed up for an ultra-marathon off the couch. Since then, Martin has won several races and has become a sponsored athlete for numerous top brands. He has wins in Swiss Canyon Trail 120km and 6000D, both in 2019. He claimed 5th in La Diagonale des Fous (La Réunion) and a solid 12th place in UTMB. A 12th place finish in UTMB in a huge achievement for anyone but for a first timer, it is an even bigger accomplishment. Pretty amazing considering that this was all achieved just four years into the sport. Who knows what Martin is capable of? Time will tell.

1. **What do you love about running and how did you get into it?**

Running gives me a lot of pleasure; being free in nature, I find my balance out there. I like challenging myself too. It is what makes it like a game and finally, I like to share my adventures with other people; it is like a team sport. I started trail running in the Pyrenees with friends who were already addicted to its benefits.

2. **Have you ever had a 'did not finish' (DNF), if so, how did you react to it?**

I experienced it once when I was a newbie (yes, we all start from somewhere). This was a 2-day race, and I could only perform one day as I had a knee injury to deal with while increasing running distances...My body was not really prepared, and I wanted to run longer distances. This was hard to accept as are all kinds of injuries, but it helped me to understand better my body limits and train differently in the future.

3. **Who are your greatest inspirations and why (either in or out of the sport)?**

I really enjoy reading books about the pioneers of alpinism such as Messner or more recently JC Lafaille and U. Steck, for example. These pioneers of extreme sports opened new doors by pushing the limits to their creativity. In trail running, I like guys like F.Dhaene or K.Jornet. Not only have they won everything in trail running, but they also constantly think out of the box and built projects that we never thought would be possible. They are always creating new ideas, projects and this is inspiring.

4. Tell us about your greatest failure?

No big failure yet, (touch wood!) But I still face difficulties in recovery times. I don't recover enough, so I am tired most of the time but hey, it is hard to stay on the couch when it is a blue-bird day outside right?

5. Tell us something interesting that not a lot of people know about you?

I like to celebrate! Most elite runners do not celebrate like I do....It is important to have a nice dinner, good drinks, and come along with great friends and share our stories.

6. How do you manage family or home life around running?

I live my life to the full, literally at 200% so between family, passions, and work, I need a solid organisation to find my balance. I can tell you that I don't go to bed very late!

7. What are your interests outside running?

Running is my own way to discover the world and find my balance. I love skiing, cycling, paragliding, and surfing. When I have some quiet time, I like to play the piano and the guitar... And I admit that cooking is as well one of my favourite interests too.

8. Do you have any race day rituals?

Yes, I do have race day rituals; it is part of my mental preparation. Everything needs to be done for me to mentally feel ready for a new big day out. Solid breakfast, day pack repack, race profile visualisation, and spend time with my favourite people around me so that I think about everything else but the race.

Instagram @kern_martin

Carla Molinaro

Carla obviously has a huge passion for endurance sports. She is a former British triathlete who turned to ultra-running and in doing so, excelled massively. Since making the switch in endurance sports, Carla has achieved vastly in numerous events, including setting a new World Record in the process. In July 2020, she set out to run Lands' End to John O'Groats (LEJOG) in a record time and she was not only successful in this attempt but smashed the previous record by more than ten hours. This is a challenge not for the faint-hearted as it entails running the whole length of the UK from bottom to top. Traditionally the event is a cycle route, but Carla completed it by foot, which means she was running around 73 miles a day for just over 12 days. Carla competes for team Great Britain in ultra-running and is a passionate advocate for strength and conditioning for runners, something that many runners often neglect. In addition to this, her ultra-journey so far has seen her win Capital to Country (69km) in 2020, setting a course record in the process and also earning a well-respected gold medal at Comrades Ultra (90km) in South Africa, where she finished in 9th place in 2018.

1. **What do you love about running and how did you get into it?**

I got into running when I was at school. I love that anyone can run, and you can do it from anywhere. It is also a great way to explore new locations!

2. **Have you ever had a 'did not finish' (DNF), if so, how did you react to it?**

I have had one and it was fine. It was because I had Plantar Fasciitis in my foot, and I physically couldn't keep on running. I always knew the race would be a risk, but I was glad that I tried it even if I couldn't get to the finish line.

3. **Who are your greatest inspirations and why (either in or out of the sport)?**

Mimi Anderson. She is an amazing ultra-runner full of life and has had some amazing results. I love her attitude towards the sport, and she has definitely inspired my journey!

4. **Tell us about your greatest failure?**

I don't think I have any failures because every time I do a race, even if it doesn't go to plan, I learn from it and figure out what went wrong and how I can better this the next time I race. Every race is a learning experience where you learn a bit more about yourself.

5. **Tell us something interesting that not a lot of people know about you?**

I was in the army for 5 years.

6. How do you manage family or home life around running?

Running is a key part of my life as I am a running coach, it is also my job; I tend to run with a lot of friends, so I use it as a way to socialise and never feel like I need to step back from running to balance things out.

7. What are your interests outside running?

I really enjoy baking and cooking. I find it really relaxing and you get something nice to eat at the end of it!

8. Do you have any race day rituals?

Not really, just have a good breakfast and I always try my hardest and see if I can push myself a little bit further!

Instagram @carlamolinaro
www.carlamolinaro.com

FOOD FOR THOUGHT

There is no doubt that athletes in all sports must go through pain and discomfort. Whether that is through training, competing, injuries, or having to cut weight for an event. The question is, do athletes have a higher pain threshold than non-athletes, are there different levels of pain thresholds across different sports, or are they all equal? Anyone who has run an ultra-marathon will know that you will at some point have a dark moment (if not several) because of physical pain in your body that you have to push through. To finish an ultra-marathon, you surely must have a strong mentality. Most people have heard these crazy stories of ultra-runners who have pushed through an event despite the body telling them to stop and not push any further. I once met a guy during an event in the Namibian desert who had one of these stories. He completed a multi-day race in Costa Rica over a five-day period and on day two, he fell over and fractured his kneecap, causing extreme pain when moving especially when running on the injury. You know how the story goes. He managed to strap up his knee with tape for the remaining three days and continue to complete the event, even though many of the other competitors were telling him to pull out of the race. Everyone will have their own opinion on this, brave or stupid? No matter what your view is on this and circumstances like this, you cannot fault the dedication and determination of people like this. Stories like this are common amongst the ultra-running world. To realise that even at a recreational level, it is not uncommon to hear ultra-runners pushing their bodies to such a degree it has to pose the question, can these athletes tolerate more pain than others?

Interestingly, Susann Dahl Pettersen (6) and her team undertook a study that suggested that elite-level athletes had higher pain tolerance across areas of heat pain thresholds and other thermal stimulation. The study suggests that the endurance athletes of the test group generally tolerated cold pain better in comparison to both non-athletes and soccer players. It could be argued that most people would have expected athletes to have a higher pain threshold mainly due to the fact that they regularly push their minds and their bodies. Brace AW, George K, and Lovell GP (7) explored this further by comparing ultra-runners with numerous other sports, including 'high level adolescent female hockey players, professional Welsh football (soccer) players, professional mixed martial artists, South African tennis players, and high-performing adolescent male athletes.' This was achieved by all athletes completing a mental toughness questionnaire. 'Mental toughness was assessed by the 14 item Sports Mental Toughness Questionnaire (SMTQ), providing an overall sports mental toughness score and three subscales; Confidence, Constancy, and Control'. The ultra-runners were selected from the HURT100 ultra held in Hawaii. The results intriguingly demonstrated the current sample of ultra-marathon runners had 'significantly and meaningfully greater mental toughness' than the other sports involved in the study. There are still a lot more studies that need to be done before drawing a conclusion. It would be great to see comparisons to many other sports to see how ultra-runners differ. Despite this, there is no doubt that people who compete in ultra-running events have a high tolerance for pain.

Tony Mangan

Tony Mangan had a very successful competitive career winning many ultra-races and proudly represented Ireland on six occasions. In addition to being the first verified runner in history to run two consecutive days of over 200 kilometres (223 and 203), he has broken four world records. Two of these he still holds as he walks around the world: He is the current world 48-hour indoor track record holder (426.178 km. He also holds the world 48-hour treadmill record, 405.22 km) This is his third time around the world, as he previously cycled it as a 22-year-old. On 27 October 2014, he achieved his life dream, to run around the world. Starting with his city marathon in Dublin on 25th October 2010, he set out to run what would eventually be a 50,000-kilometre lap around the world. In all, he ran across 41 countries, including North and South America, New Zealand, Australia, Asia, and Europe. After a lap of Ireland, he finished his world run where he started, at the finish line of the Dublin Marathon. Retired from running in February 2016, he set out from Dublin to walk around the world. By March 2019, he had walked almost 34,000 kilometres across Europe, Russia, China, Mongolia and South-East Asia, Australia, and New

Zealand. In 2019 he backtracked on his route to walk 'extra distance' in Africa, Saudi Arabia, and the Arabian Gulf. Due to Covid-19 pandemic and logistical issues, including border closures, he has been forced to pause his walk. Since March 2020, he has been resting in Zanzibar and Kenya, waiting for the opportunity to get back on the road.

Anthony Rogan

1. What do you love about running and how did you get into it?

I love the freedom of running. I truly believe that one of the great benefits of sport is therapeutic. The mental feel-good benefits of a relaxing run, walk or even a leisurely cycle is a joy to behold, and I encourage anyone with difficult issues in their life to put some time aside and try it. There were times in the past when I was feeling down and once, I tied up my running shoes and went running in my local park that wherever worries or aggressions I had previously seemed to dissipate. I was a late starter as I only started running a few months before my 30th birthday. For many years after watching the first Dublin City Marathons live on Irish television, I developed a fascination with marathon running. Before that, I was slow to take to it. For a couple of years, I promised myself to go out and do a training run before the year's end. I remember one year not going out until the evening of New Year's Eve, just to keep that promise to myself. I then got into more serious running in September 1986. Looking back, I got caught up in the running boom of that time. I entered a 10K fun run which was sponsored by Radio Nova. They gave it great hype and made it fun. By the time I crossed the finish line, I decided that I would run the Dublin Marathon as it was only 6 weeks away. I figured that way, I would take care of one of my lifetime ambitions and I would probably never run again. That way, I would not have to do the months of training required and running would be 'done and dusted' from my life quicker than it had started! Leading up to that day, I ran my only long run of 35 kilometres seven days before my 3:09 marathon debut. Much to my surprise, I then got hooked and entered every fun run I could find! In those days I also used to play a lot of football. The proverbial penny only dropped when I got an ankle injury and much to my astonishment, after a few weeks of inactivity, I missed running more than the footie. Besides, I was an appalling football player—I haven't kicked a competitive ball since. My then girlfriend's boss was on the committee of Metropolitan Harriers, a Dublin-based running club. So, I joined them in January 1987. For a few years, I ran 10-kilometre and marathon events and concentrated on getting my times down to 33 minutes and 2:38, respectively. My ambition for several years was to try to win the Finglas Marathon. I had several placings in the top three to six but never managed to win it. In 1994 I emigrated to the Colorado Rockies in the United States and I loved it. I ran many mountain races and that's where I discovered ultra-running. I soon discovered I could compete in ultras. The longer the distance, the better I ran and the more competitive I became... In 2002, due to a plantar fasciitis injury, I returned to Dublin for treatment. This injury usually takes about six months to recover from. However, Michael Farrell, my physio, was so good he had me back running in two months. I ended up staying in Ireland. I continued running ultras, focusing mostly on the 24 and 48-hour events. Many years before and during a lap of Dublin's Phoenix Park, I dreamt of the mad notion of running around the world. Immediately, I become a prisoner of that dream as there was barely a waking hour that I didn't think about it or research my route in my head.

2. **Have you ever had a 'did not finish' (DNF), if so, how did you react to it?**

I have had a handful of DNF's but always because of injury and never because I couldn't be bothered to finish a race, or I wasn't going to hit my distance or race position target. I usually just dusted my mind down with the thought that my effort was a good workout for my next effort. To me, every race experience is like an ingredient one can add to a stew. It all adds up to the end product and will come good in the end.

3. **Who are your greatest inspirations and why (either in or out of the sport)?**

My two greatest inspirations are both women. Firstly, Dervla Murphy is an Irish author and adventurer extraordinaire. After reading her book 'Full Tilt—Ireland To India On A Bicycle.' It was a hair-raising cycle which she completed in the 1960s. Back then, roads, equipment and indeed bicycles were not as good as they are today. I was so inspired that I read the book three times within a couple of weeks and then went out and bought a bicycle. Soon after that, I was planning my own India cycle. However, as I am not a man to do things in half-measures, there seemed little point in cycling halfway around the world and cycling or flying back. It was then that my dream to cycle around the world was born. Also, Rosie Swale-Pope, who though in her mid-seventies is still running around the world and putting her great efforts into fundraising for needy charities. She makes her trips on a shoestring and generally shuns luxuries preferring to camp in cold weather. Just take a look at Rosie's Facebook page and I guarantee you that her latest posts will always have an upbeat, positive, warm-hearted, loving feel. She is a genuine real-life role model. There have been times when I have been angry with some people or some issues that I have had and found myself asking what Rosie would have done or said in this situation. After reading The Man Who Walked Around the World by David Kunst and Steven Newman's World Walk, I was further inspired to run and walk around the world.

4. Tell us something interesting that not a lot of people know about you?

Sadly, though I'm not sure if you would classify it as interesting but… I'm a talk show junkie and listen to way too many than what's healthy for my head! As far back as the late eighties and nineties, I was recording my favourite talk shows. Even the late-night ones, I had my recorder set up to turn on with a socket timer! So, you can imagine how I am today with podcasts.

5. How do you manage family or home life around running?

Not surprisingly, with all of the travelling and training for my ultra-races, I'm single! In Dublin, I worked in construction and most days, I ran into work and then I ran back home. At that time, I had a girlfriend who lived on the opposite side of Dublin, where I once lived. A couple of times a week, I got my training in by running to her house and then after a shower and a change of clothes, we went out for the evening. Then I ran to work in the morning. There were countless long gruelling days on the site when the last thing that I wanted to do was to run home. Those distances varied from 5-15 kilometres and what I was doing was developing coping strategies. At that job, we didn't work on Saturdays and I had my training and a heavy social weekend planned out. Most importantly I just had to get in vital back-to-back 35-kilometre-long slow distance runs that Saturday and Sunday. Suddenly, on Friday afternoon, I was asked to work that Saturday morning for an urgent job. As I was an agency worker, I couldn't refuse. How would I fit in Saturday's long run? That Friday evening I was going to a rock concert and I had already paid for my ticket. I could have missed the concert…But still!! There was a vital Ireland Six Nations rugby match on Saturday afternoon. I could have missed that, but…Still! A couple of hours after the rugby I was meeting my girlfriend but… Still! Anyway, I wasn't in her good books as she wasn't impressed after reading my recent answer to a… 'What's your best advice to an ultra-runner?' question in a newspaper interview. My advice to that question was that if running or something else is important to you, to make it the most important part of your life! I know that's hard for most people. Anyway, after the rock concert on Friday evening, I went straight home and set the alarm clock for 4 AM and ran my 35-kilo-metre training run from my house near the South Circular Road to my job site in Dun Laoghaire via some laps of the Phoenix Park. I arrived at the site ten minutes early and after a quick change, I was breaking my back with a hammer drill! All worked out well that weekend!

How did other people react to your excessive running? (Additional question added in by Tony)
Because I ran in and out of work on my construction site, I was often the butt of many jokes. Some of my workmates

teased me by wondering how I could run to work and then do such a physical job. Often, when I was changing in the dressing room to run home, the joke was that I must not have worked hard as otherwise, I wouldn't have the energy to run home. As I was an agency worker, I needed to be careful that that joke didn't get back to my agency office. My solution was to work harder than others so as nobody could make any serious allegations. Of course, my family, close friends and those close to me in work understood my passion and drive and were always supportive. Funny enough, some of my best supporters were the managers and supervisors on some of the construction sites where I got the most ribbing from my workmates. A great memory I have after breaking the world 48-hour indoor track record in Brno, Czech Republic, in March 2007. The race ended on a Sunday, I travelled home the next day and I was at work that Tuesday morning. Nobody knew about my record-breaking race, except for my supervisor. We had a quick chat and congrats and after assuring me that I had my eyes in the back of my head and that I looked fuc**d up, he told me to go to the top of the apartment block that we were building and to sit in a room reading a paper and listening to the radio for a couple of days and that he would call me if the project manager was doing his rounds.

6. What are your interests outside running?

Travelling. I have found a way to marry my three great loves of cycling, running, and walking with travelling around the world using those modes. I just love stopping in cafes and grocery stores in way out places between villages and talking to people and also when they stop on the road to talk to me. Also, for almost fifty years, I am a passionate Liverpool supporter and rarely miss their games.

7. Do you have any race day rituals?

Other than running to races, not much. Except on one occasion. At a 48-hour road race in America. I put a 4x4 wheel drive toy truck on my aid station table as a motivation factor! In previous events in Europe and the USA, I had already achieved 400 kilometres plus in three of the four 48-hour surfaces (indoor track, outdoor track, and treadmill) All that I needed to complete the set of 4x4 was the outdoor road 400-kilometre distance and I was there to give it my best shot… Unfortunately, despite winning that race, I fell short.

www.theworldjog.com/
www.facebook.com/tony.mangan.14
theworldjog@gmail.com

Hallvard Schjølberg

After reaching 100kg in bodyweight, Hallvard started running to lose the excess weight and now he is a running machine. With a little help from his daughter, who signed him and his wife up for the Oslo Marathon in 2011, he now boasts of numerous successes in the ultra-world. In 2018 he placed 4th at the UTMB 171 kilometres race and in 2018, he repeated his 4th place finish in the TDS race at UTMB. On top of this, he claimed 1st at Innsbruck Alpine Trailrun Festival 85k in 2019 and 1st in the National Ultra Trail Championship in 2018. He won the Arctic Triple—Lofoten Ultra-Trail 100 miler three years in a row from 2016 to 2018. Hallvard also has two second-place finishes at Oslo Ecotrail 80k in 2016 and 2017.

1. What do you love about running and how did you get into it?

I was 100 kilograms, and I had a very unhealthy lifestyle. Then my daughter signed me and my wife up for the Oslo marathon in 2011. We started running and we enjoyed our new hobby and really liked the racing atmosphere, so I challenged myself to get better every year. In 2015 I heard of a race called UTMB and Western States, it really fascinated me, and I started running in the terrain to see what it was like. First, the motivation was to only lose weight; after some years, the biggest motivation is to challenge myself to race big ultra-races. It is good to be out in the mountains, enjoy nature and make nice memories.

2. Have you ever had a 'did not finish' (DNF), if so, how did you react to it?

I have not had a DNF…yet.

3. Who are your greatest inspirations and why (either in or out of the sport)?

People who arrange running events for us to play and have fun. Without those guys, the events would not happen.

4. Tell us about your greatest failure?

I learnt a lot from the Ecotrail 80k Madeira as I started way too fast. It was a very hot day, and the sun was blazing. The trails were very steep and because I went out too fast, I had to walk the last 60km, but I learnt a good lesson for future races.

5. Tell us something interesting that not a lot of people know about you?

I have 3-5 months with almost no running during winter, just skiing a bit when there is good weather.

6. How do you manage family or home life around running?

I often train late in the evenings/night when the kids are asleep.

7. What are your interests outside running?

I like to go fishing in my spare time and enjoy woodworking.

8. Do you have any race day rituals?

After I finish a race, I like to have a beer, dry fish and ice cream. Before racing, I don't have any rituals and don't really warm up; it works for me.

Instagram @hallvard_schjolberg

Patrick Reagan

As a professional ultra-runner and running coach, there is not a lot that Patrick has not experienced in the world of running. In 2017 he was named USATF Ted Corbitt Ultra runner of the Year, an award that only a few are honoured with receiving. As an athlete himself, he has several career highlights, including three first-place wins at Javelina Jundred 100 miler on the bounce from 2017 to 2019. This includes setting a course record in 2017 with a time of 13:01:14. Yes, you read that right, 100 miles in just over 13 hours. In addition to this, in 2016, he finished 3rd in the IAU 100k World Championships and has had successes all over the world. As a coach, Patrick mostly focuses on people who are training for ultra-marathons. However, he has also coached cross country and track & field collegiately. Patrick has received awards in his time coaching by being named The Sun Conference Coach of the year on six occasions, four for the women's team and twice for the men's team.

1. What do you love about running and how did you get into it?

Running for me has been a vessel of personal exploration of my physical limitations. Through sport, I've developed discipline and been humbled on so many occasions. In Ultrarunning, I've met most of my closest friends and embraced the importance of the community aspect of our sport. I became a runner at the age of 14, after spending most of my younger years playing basketball, skateboarding, getting super into punk rock music, and riding BMX bicycles. My dad encouraged my interest in track and field in high school which lead to cross country, which helped to fund my education at university via Cross Country scholarships.

2. Have you ever had a 'did not finish' (DNF), if so, how did you react to it?

The only DNF I've had (which is not actually considered a DNF because it was in a timed race) is in the 2018 Desert Solstice 24 Hour Track Invitational. I stepped off the track at about 18 hours with 125 miles and later walked an additional 5. The event impacted me in a negative way at the time, but I feel as though I learned about the importance of developing a plan for unexpected circumstances.

3. Who are your greatest inspirations and why (either in or out of the sport)?

My mom/dad, nana/papa, and grandma raised me and taught me to be the best human I could be. In the sport, Zach Bitter, Madga Boulet, and Ian Sharman have been great mentors and friends.

4. Tell us about your greatest failure?

I consider the 2018 Desert Solstice 24 Hour Invitational to be a failure that taught me the importance of perseverance and troubleshooting. The outcome of that event taught me to not quit when things get tough but to instead pivot nutrition and implement massage/mobility work when needed to get to the finish line.

5. Tell us something interesting that not a lot of people know about you?

After graduating from university, I played washboard percussion/tenor banjo in string bands in Pittsburgh, New Orleans, and Savannah.

6. How do you manage family or home life around running?

Balance is an important aspect of being a professional athlete. My wife, our pets, and I make sure to go into each day with the intent to have fun and live in the moment outside of running and work. We have a healthy love for art, music, and the outdoors. Athletic performance is only one part of the puzzle for me.

7. What are your interests outside running?

All sorts of music, especially Punk Rock, Trad Jazz, Pre-WW2 Jug Band/Hot Jazz/Blues, and Post Rock. Science Fiction and Fantasy Novels. Riding Bikes. Kayaking. I play about 2 hours of music a day solo and with my friends.

8. Do you have any race day rituals?

My mantra and only ritual: Keep Running, keep Eating, keep Smiling.

Instagram @patrickreaganrunning
www.patrickreaganrunning.com
Twitter @preagan
Podcast: Tortoise & The Hare Podcast
My New Band's Instagram @doctorraygunand
thefuturetimes

Anthony Rogan

Isis Breiter

sis's running journey all started with taunts from her husband, he was a regular runner, but she wasn't very good at the time, so she started training with the initial goal of being better than him. The goal started with wanting to be better than her husband, but it grew quickly with her setting her sights on running Marathon Des Sables, no easy task by any means. Several years later, the mother of four children has run and won some of the most brutal races on the globe. This includes becoming the first Mexican person and Hispanic woman to win the 4 Deserts Grand Slam. This event consists of four 250-kilometre races around the world, including Atacama Crossing (Chile), Gobi March (Mongolia), Namib Race (Namibia) and The Last Desert (Antarctica). Pretty impressive considering that Isis did not started running until her 30s proving that it is never too late to start running. She is also a motivational speaker.

1. **What do you love about running and how did you get into it?**

What I love most about running is the time I have for myself; while I run, I reflect on many things. I started in my 30s as a personal challenge because I had tried it before, in my opinion I was not made to run and I abandoned it at two kilometres, until one day I did not get off the tread-mill until I finished four kms and I was surprised by that distance. For me it was a lot, I thought if I can run four, I think I can run six, so I increased the distance and ended up being really passionate about running.

2. **Have you ever had a 'did not finish' (DNF), if so, how did you react to it?**

There was a race in China that was to run 400 km nonstop and at kilometre 90, I collapsed, and I couldn't run anymore and when they found me, I had hypothermia. That was my first race of not finishing; it was a strange feeling because at the same time, I was lucky not to continue because it endangered my life. I was happy that they found me on time because we were running in the desert and every 50 kms there was a check-point. On the other hand, I had trained so much for that race that not finishing was sad, it was something crazy that time.

3. **Who are your greatest inspirations and why (either in or out of the sport)?**

My children inspire me to run because I am their role model. Also, all the runners that are moms inspire me. Dean Karnazes inspires me in what it is to run, I think he's a great runner.

4. Tell us about your greatest failure?

I learnt the hard way but to think that I can run without drinking water for a long time and then I end up dizzy. Please don't do it and carry a lot of water both in training and competitions.

5. Tell us something interesting that not a lot of people know about you?

I am extremely crazy to sleep ten continuous hours because for me, rest is the most important thing. Also, I have 15 different allergies and sometimes that complicates things when I am running.

6. How do you manage family or home life around running?

It's complicated, being a mommy, working, training, traveling, it gets a little crazy at the beginning, but with schedules set, it is easier. I think I'm lucky because my family supports me a lot on that issue when I go to compete outside of Mexico.

7. What are your interests outside running?

I give motivational talks at conferences in hotels and universities. Almost everything I do revolves around running.

8. Do you have any race day rituals?

Not really, I just try to have fun running when I race.

Instagram @isis_breiter

Lucy Bartholomew

Finishing an ultra-event is impressive no matter what the age, but imagine completing a 100km race at fifteen and running it with your Dad; pretty cool I would say. There aren't a lot of people who can brag about that. Fast forward several years, most people on their 21st birthday would be out celebrating with drinks, not Lucy. She was busy winning one of her local ultra-races, the Ultra-Trail Australia 100km and setting a course record in the process. In her first attempt at the prestigious Western States 100-mile Endurance Run, she placed 3rd after leading the race at the 100km point. In addition to this, Lucy has run all over the world, including the Alps of France, a 250km race in the Simpson desert and the coastlines of South Africa, to name a few. This girl seems to have ultra-running in the palms of her hands, and it will be exciting to see what she can achieve in this astounding sport.

1. What do you love about running and how did you get into it?

I got into running with my dad when I was 15. It was never about the actual act of running or the numbers; it was about spending time with him, going away to amazing places, the food afterwards and the stories I would go to school the next day and tell. I love the freedom of running, the open and raw conversations you can have and the empowering feeling of seeing where you have come from with your own two feet.

2. Have you ever had a 'did not finish' (DNF), if so, how did you react to it?

I have and I am sure I will again. In the running world, it seems like a bad thing to 'DNF' but instead, I look at it like, "at least I tried, and now I learnt something."

3. Who are your greatest inspirations and why (either in or out of the sport)?

For sure, my dad is my biggest inspiration as I see him get up and at it every day. I also draw inspiration from the people I meet along my travels and conversations; the parents, full-time workers, the injury over-comers, the dreamers- anyone who dares to be uncomfortable in pursuit of learning something is an inspiration to me.

4. Tell us about your greatest failure?

I don't really like the word failure; I choose to call it learnings. For a period of time, I lost the respect for running and took it for granted. I had always said that when I outran my love of running, I would stop. I did that, yet I tried to force it and push through.

5. Tell us something interesting that not a lot of people know about you?

I have never lost a toenail. In 9 years of ultra-running!!

6. How do you manage family or home life around running?

I run professionally but that doesn't mean that there isn't balance in social and family life. I run my best when I am happy and that means spending time with my family and friends, being flexible in my schedule and prioritising what excites me. It ebbs and flows with the racing calendar, but I have amazing friends and family who know that no race will ever mean as much as them and support me to chase my dreams.

7. What are your interests outside running?

I just love being outside and moving. It doesn't have to be running. I balance that with spending time in the kitchen and creating plant-based meals to share, reading, or playing with my dog (or any animal that comes near me!). I play hard and I rest harder.

8. Do you have any race day rituals?

I love to braid my hair for big races. I feel like it sets me up for success. Such a funny thing since I don't care for my hair any other day of the year but "look good, feel good, run good" is my mentality!

Instagram @lucy_bartholomew
www.lucybartholomew.com

John Maxwell

For most people driving 200 miles is a hard enough task without stopping for a break. Try running that distance and see how it feels; it is not for the faint hearted. John took on the Moab 240 in 2019, finishing an impressive 8th place in his first time running the 238-mile distance. This meant he was running for a total of 76 hours 22 minutes and 57 seconds. Let's just stop and think about just how insane that is. Moreover, he has a couple of podium finishes in other distances such as 50k and 50 miles. Additionally, he finished an impressive 8th in the Tillamook 50 miler in 2021 and 9th in the 2018 Pine to Palm 100 miler. Clearly, John can perform at any distance when it comes to ultra-running. He had a huge year in 2018, as well as his notable performances in 2018 saw him run a total of 2,915 miles and he ran in five different countries. In 2019 he set a new Unsupported FKT on the 93-mile Wonderland Trail (WA), with his second attempt showing that persistence pays off.

1. **What do you love about running and how did you get into it?**

I love running for the places, people, and experiences it's allowed me to enjoy. If I travel someplace new, I'm always looking for trails to explore or running groups to meet up with. Although just as much as I enjoy the social aspect, I enjoy the alone time. If I'm in a funk or just need/want to de-stress, running is my first outlet of choice. I first got into running back in college (not a college runner) to stay in shape. But as time went on and I got in better shape, I realised I could run a lot further than I ever thought. It's one of those sports that you have to put in the work, no shortcuts and can then clearly see the benefits. It's amazing to see what your body can do once you put your mind to it. And I plan to find out how far I can push my limits.

2. **Have you ever had a 'did not finish' (DNF), if so, how did you react to it?**

Although I haven't had an official DNF in a race, there are two instances that stand out to me where I had to quit a run without getting to my goal. The first one was in 2019 when I attempted the Wonderland Unsupported FKT. 30 miles into it, I started feeling "off" and by mile 60, I knew it wasn't my day. I called it quits and had to find a ride back to my car but that ignited a fire in me to get out there and finish what I had started. It was all I could think about and knew I could do it. So, 7-days later, I was back out there, completed the loop and got the new Unsupported FKT. The second DNF was last year (2020) when I attempted the WA PCT FKT. Long story short it was rough! But after 400 miles an Achilles injury forced me to stop. It was extremely tough to quit after 6-days on the trail but similar to Wonderland, it drove me to train smarter, work hard and then just a week ago I was able to set my new 100mile PB.

3. Who are your greatest inspirations and why (either in or out of the sport)?

Steve Prefontaine was my original inspiration to get into running. The way he raced and the drive he had to do his best was incredible. It made me think about all the times I had given up on sports because it got tough. Or when I would stop running because I "thought" I was tired. Pre's mindset was STRONG and what I've come to find out is that if you set your mind to it and give yourself no excuses, you can push boundaries you never thought possible.

4. Tell us about your greatest failure?

My greatest failure has to do with running but not as you may think. When I started getting into ultra-running, I started putting running over almost all aspects of life. I would run in the morning, during work if I could, after work, in the middle of the night etc. I wanted to get into the best physical running shape I could. But what that led to was me putting my family in the backseat. I ran on holidays, birthdays; you name it. I was physically strong but mentally struggling with my family not supporting my passion. It took a lot of work to find the balancing point and it wasn't easy, but we did it together and now I couldn't be happier.

5. Tell us something interesting that not a lot of people know about you?

Growing up in the PNW, I thought this place was terrible. It was cold, rained a lot, and in the winter it gets dark by 4pm. It actually wasn't until running that I started shifting that mindset and really enjoying the great northwest. Temperature is perfect for running year-round without much change in clothing. The mountains and oceans so close are just beautiful and running in the dark is one of my favourite times to run. So, it goes to show you that so much of life is about perspective. Sometimes you just need to step back and take a new look.

6. How do you manage family or home life around running?

Like I mentioned a little above, balancing family and running was difficult at first. But I've learned to be flexible, run early in the morning while the family is sleeping and be "ok" when I miss a day of training due to life's unexpectedness. That being said, my family is absolutely amazing and fully supportive of my running aspirations, which is critical if someone plans to spend a lot of time away from the family running. Another way I've managed it is by including my family in my training. Sometimes that means pushing my boys in the jogging stroller; other times, incorporating running into a family outing. The key is finding what best works for your family and be open to change on the fly.

7. What are your interests outside running?

Family, friends and almost anything in the outdoors. I love camping, hiking, going to the beach, snowboarding, boating etc. I also really enjoy a good beer and tend to incorporate stops at local breweries very frequently.

8. Do you have any race day rituals?

The day before a race is probably the most critical for me. I like to take a 30-minute jog to relax any race nerves, rest, hydrate and then take some time to ensure I'm packed and talk aid station plans over with my wife. Then I normally enjoy a single IPA before going to bed. On race day, I'm just ready to go. I eat food I know will sit well in my stomach and then get to the start line. Once there, I like to look around and strategize a bit. Will I run fast off the start, hang back a little, run with a friend etc. All depends on my goals and length of race.

Instagram @run_john

Mark Hammond

There aren't many ultra-races that Mark would not sign up for; he gets stuck in seeing every race to push himself and develop as a runner. He is definitely amongst the top ultra-runners in the USA, if not the world. He has shown this by finishing 3rd twice in the legendry Western States 100 and with a 5th place finish in 2019. His 5th place finish time of 15:36:12 in 2019 means that he is in the top twenty in the men's category for the fastest times in the forty-plus year history of the Western States 100. Mark has a passion for anything outdoors, not just ultra-running. His other outdoor pursuits include mountaineering, rock climbing, and backcountry skiing. In 2016 he hiked and skied the highest peak in each county in Utah. In 2020 Mark also set a new FKT on the Wonderland Trail WA, which was unsupported. He podiums frequently in races that he enters in all kinds of distances, including 50km, 100km, 100 miles, and 24-hour races. It will be exciting watching Marks' career to see what else he is capable of.

Anthony Rogan

1. **What do you love about running and how did you get into it?**

I love running because it's so simple and practical. You can do it no matter where you live or what your economic circumstances are. It's a great sport, a convenient way to exercise, and fun method of transportation. It enables you to explore wild places in an environmentally sustainable way. Traveling faster through the wilderness can simplify the logistics of the outing. I wasn't involved in competitive running during high school or college. During that time, I primarily developed my aerobic fitness through ski touring and mountaineering. I've been trail running occasionally since I was a teenager, but I didn't get serious about running until my late 20s when I started doing little runs around my office building during lunch breaks. I gradually added mileage and workouts to those lunch runs until I felt confident enough to enter some races. I soon got into ultras because I already had a big aerobic base from ski touring and mountaineering.

2. **Have you ever had a 'did not finish' (DNF), if so, how did you react to it?**

I've had 10 DNFs out of about 100 races. I've never DNFed because I absolutely had to drop out because of some medical reason. It's always happened when I get to a point in a race when I know my performance won't be anywhere near what I was hoping for and I don't want to beat myself up anymore just for the sake of finishing. I've already finished plenty of races. I'd rather cut my losses and focus on recovering for the next race.

3. Who are your greatest inspirations and why (either in or out of the sport)?

My greatest inspirations are master's athletes (40+ yrs old) who are still performing at an elite level. I highly respect the dedication and wisdom they demonstrate in defying their age. They give me hope that I can run well for a couple more decades.

4. Tell us about your greatest failure?

Perhaps my greatest failure was the 2018 UTMB. I trained very well for that race and was near the top 10 for over 60 miles. However, I really screwed up my nutrition which led to me dropping out around mile 70. That was a blown opportunity to perform well on the biggest stage in trail running. The silver lining of dropping out was I saved enough energy to take 2nd place at Run Rabbit Run 100 just two weeks later.

5. Tell us something interesting that not a lot of people know about you?

I'm an avid fly fisherman. I started fly fishing when I was 12, long before I got into athletics. It's my favourite rest day activity.

6. How do you manage family or home life around running?

The only way I've found to balance running with family life is to use my home treadmill for much of my training. My job allows me to work remotely and I have an improvised treadmill desk so I can get some work done while jogging. Balancing running with work and family is only getting harder as I have more kids, but I enjoy the challenge.

7. What are your interests outside running?

Aside from ski touring and fly fishing, my other favourite non-running sport is rock climbing. That was the first sport I really got into when I was a teenager. It's a fun way to stretch my legs after a big run.

8. Do you have any race day rituals?

Not really. I just wake 90 minutes before the race and drink some chocolate milk.

Instagram @mark.d.hammond

Carol Seppilu

his is someone that I had to leave until last to feature in the book. Although she is not an 'elite' runner nor is she claiming to be, she is the definition of what ultra-running is about. Carol's story is an inspiring one and she has all the traits for ultra-running. For those that are not in the know, Carol at the age of sixteen, attempted suicide. Whilst intoxicated, she shot herself in the face and since the incident, she was left with injuries that make it difficult to talk and breathe. Her running journey started after years of operations, lack of exercise and depression. Running now contributes to her daily life and helps her overcome her mental health problems. Since she started running, she has run numerous ultra-distances, including Resurrection Pass Ultras 50 miler, North Face Challenge Utah 50K, Bandera 50K (broke her ankle at mile 5 and still finished it), and Resurrection Pass 100 miler, plus many more. It is incredible to see some of the feats that the elite runners can do but most of us (including me) will be running in the middle or the back of the pack. However, the sport of ultra-running has many elements such as dedication, pushing through pain thresholds, and discipline to name a few. Carol has these traits in abundance and her pursuit to become an ultra-runner is not only amazing to see but inspiring as well. This story has many elements to it but shows that we can all keep going and pushing to be better people and athletes. It is exactly like an ultra-race, there will be times that you want to quit and think that you cannot continue but once you do it, there will be the most rewarding feeling. Carol shows that we can all test our boundaries further than we could ever imagine and not be frightened to achieve what we want.

1. **What do you love about running and how did you get into it?**

On a beautiful summer day in 2014, I found myself lying in bed at noon thinking, "Carol, you need to get up and do something. Go for a 2-mile run." I was 233 lbs and depressed. I could only run a couple of blocks, but I made the decision to walk the rest of the way. It was my goal to do this every day. After about a year, those two blocks turned into a mile of running, and a mile turned into a few. Seeing how much farther I can go became an obsession, even to this day. I love how running makes me feel happier and healthier.

2. **Have you ever had a 'did not finish' (DNF), if so, how did you react to it?**

My first attempt at an ultramarathon was a DNF. I had planned on signing up for a 50K in Utah while visiting close friends, but I didn't know these types of races can fill up. I was too late to enter the 50K, so I decided I'd do the 100K and do half of it. I was very proud to have done over 50K, so it wasn't such a big disappointment for me. I had fun. I also signed up for a 100 miler later that year without understanding elevation gain because who knew massively hilly races existed. The hills are small at the Hitchcock Endurance 100 miler in Iowa but it's a little more than 20,000 ft of gain. I made it halfway and told them I had the heart but not the body. I've been going back every year ever since then, trying to finish it. Tough race. But I'm determined to get it done because I like to finish what I started. I got lost a couple of times at another 50K in Utah and I called the race director to ask for directions. He told me to stay put, came and got me, and pulled me out. I was a little disappointed cause I knew I had it, but now we're good friends.

3. Who are your greatest inspirations and why (either in or out of the sport)?

In the sport, I am greatly inspired by Courtney Dauwalter. She loves to go far and smiles through it. Someday I want to be as good of a long-distance runner as her. I draw inspiration from my ancestors. They were very strong and resilient people who worked hard to survive harsh conditions. Whenever I feel like I'm having it tough, I think about them. I often feel connected to their spirits when I run far. My mother is also my inspiration. She is a faithful woman who has lovingly provided for us. Today she has a tough time walking, but you can see her out and about all the time on her jogger stroller that she uses for support.

4. Tell us about your greatest failure?

It unexpectedly snowed 9 inches at the 2018 Hitchcock Endurance 100 miler. I was trained for a snowy run. There I am, the only Alaskan in the race, racing among the top in women, and my feet were in bad shape because I didn't have the right gear. It was tough to make the decision to pull myself out after 85 miles and over 18,000 ft of gain well before cut-off time. It was very bittersweet. I was proud to have made it far, but it wasn't enough but now, I make sure to bring all sorts of gear to races in case the weather decides to surprise us again.

5. Tell us something interesting that not a lot of people know about you?

I'm very introverted. It may not seem like it because I like to share a lot of my life on social media. But I share my life in hopes that it will save others. Sometimes I'll go quiet and want to disappear, but the messages people send keep me motivated. It touches me when others say I inspired them in their own journey.

6. How do you manage family or home life around running?

I don't have a family of my own, so it's easy for me to have time for lots of running. I do make sure I visit family and friends though, cause they're important to me.

7. What are your interests outside running?

I love my native culture. We carry on the traditions of our ancestors, and I have a passion for Eskimo dancing. It's dance to the music of traditional drums and singing. I also love to gather food from the land.

8. Do you have any race day rituals?

I love to eat oatmeal and orange when I wake up on race day. I also pray for a safe race.

Instagram @nasqaq

FINAL THOUGHTS

When you have completed a run or endurance challenge, you always look back and think, 'could I have done better.' This is the same with any project we take on, including this book for me. The big question for me is, did I achieve what I set out to achieve? The answer to that is yes and so much more that I could not have anticipated. When I set out to write this book, I expected that the stories from the different ultra-runners would be inspirational, and I hope that you will agree some of these tails and thoughts are incredibly inspiring. What I didn't fully anticipate however was how much this inspiration would be applicable to life in general. There is no doubt that these athletes are special; however, they also show that hard work, dedication, and discipline get you to a lot of places, including in everyday life. Even the project of writing this. Hearing different athletes' views on perceived failures is eye-opening and has taught me that if we learn from the experience, then it is worth it. The real failure is from not trying at all and I am not just talking about racing. What you can learn from these athletes is that if you apply yourself in any project in life, you can be successful. I cannot think of many people who enjoy doing something that they are not good at, but we admire people who give it their best and do not quit.

One of my favourite quotes from the book is from Ryno Greisel who said, "the more you quit, the easier it is to justify quitting." I couldn't agree more; we all know a person who cannot apply themselves to anything they do and struggle to progress. I know several people myself who have this quitting mindset and unfortunately struggle to progress in all aspects of their lives, from training, jobs, and relationships. A quitting culture as Ryno highlights, is not a good place to be as it will justify quitting no matter the project. These athletes show on numerous occasions that they are successful in a lot of aspects of their lives, not just in their running careers. If they are not professional runners, then they are living a life of success in their field and a life of fulfilment as they are chasing what they want to do. I think there is a lot of people in the world doing things that they do not want to do and that can lead to unhappiness. One of the main things I have taken from these inspiring group of runners is that there is a clear connection that they are doing what they want to do and not leading a life of regrets. If you have a goal, do not let anything stop you in your way.

Another common theme amongst the athletes is that they love to see running in the mountains and outdoors as a way of exploration and adventure. One of the main reasons why I love the outdoors is to explore new places and the excitement of discovering something new, something most of the working adult world has lost. The world is only becoming less active and increasing levels of obesity emphasise this. We now live in a world that is increasingly becoming less active and less adventurous. I think Damian Hall puts it perfectly by stating "I love the sense of adventure you can get with it, running in the mountains is exciting. I guess they are safe adventures." We are gradually losing that connection with moving our bodies and rates of disease growing year on year is a clear indication of this. I think it is time we address this situation and move our bodies more and what better way to do this than exploring some of nature's best playgrounds, the mountains. It appears that many people are frightened to try things new in case of 'failure,' but from my own life experiences, I can honestly say when I have not achieved what I set out to, I had the most growth from that situation, I am sure many of you can also relate to this. I think Hanny Allston hits the nail on the head when saying, "If we only succeeded, we would truly miss out on these valuable learning experiences." So, let's stop being frightened of perceived failures and start saying yes to more challenges physically and academically and live life to the full. I'd love to have featured more of the many great ultra-runners out there but I am immensely grateful to all those who contributed. You are all inspirational and each runner has contributed something unique and added a different perspective to the book. For those that felt that they should have been included, or to the reader who considers a great ultra-runner has been missed in this addition, my apologies for the omission. No slight was intended, and I hope in any future project, we will cross paths. I don't know about you, but I am off for a run.

DETAILS OF RACES

Name of race	Distance	Approx. Date	Elevation (Approx.)	Place of race
Western States	100.2 miles	Late June	18,090 feet (5500m)	California Sierra Nevada
UTMB OCC	56 km	August	3500 metres	Orsières, Switzerland
UTMB TDS	121 km	August	7,300 metres	Courmayeur, Italy
UTMB CCC	101 km	August	6,100 metres	Courmayeur, Italy
UTMB Ultra-Trail du Mont-Blanc	171 km	August	10,040 metres	Chamonix Mont-Blanc, France
Hardrock 100	100.5 miles	July	33,000 feet (10,000m)	Colorado
HURT 100	100 miles	January	24,000 feet	Island of O'ahu, Hawai
Ultra-Trail Mt. Fuji	168 km	April	9,500 metres	Yamanashi Prefecture and Shizuoka Prefecture, Japan
Ultra X Sri Lanka	250 km 5 stage multi day race	March	687 metres	Udawalawe National Park, Sri Lanka

Anthony Rogan

Name of race	Distance	Approx. Date	Elevation (Approx.)	Place of race
Wasatch 100	100 miles	First Friday and Saturday after Labor Day each year	24,000 feet	Utah, USA
Pennine Way (FKT)	268 miles	N/A	12,000 metres	England/ Scottish borders
Paddy Buckley Round (FKT)	100 km	N/A	8,500 metres	Wales
The Spine Race	268 miles	English winter-time	13,300 metres	England/ Scotland
Montane Dragons Back Race	380 km 6-day multi-stage race	September	17,400 metres	Wales
Marathon Des Sables (MDS)	251 km 6-day multi-stage race	April	1000 metres	Sahara Desert, Southern Morocco
The Atacama Crossing Race	250 km 6 stage multiday race	September -October	1,683 metres	Chile

Name of race	Distance	Approx. Date	Elevation (Approx.)	Place of race
Salomon Cappadocia Ultra-Trail	119 km	October	3730 metres	Turkey
Lake Sonoma 50	50 miles	April	10,500 feet	California
Way to cool 50k	50 km	March	4,839 feet	Sierra Nevada
Bandera Endurance Run	100 km	January	10,844 feet	Bandera, USA near San Antonio
Ultra-Trail Austra-lia 100 (UTA100)	100 km	May	4460 metres	Katoomba, New South Wales, Australia
Ultra-Trail Australia 50 (UTA50)	50.3 km	May	2450 metres	Katoomba, New South Wales, Australia
Javelina Jundred	100 miles and 100 km	October	7,900 feet for 100 miles and 5,000 feet for 100 km	Arizona
Comrades	90 km	May/June	7,000 feet	Durban/Piet-ermaritzburg, South Africa
Two Oceans Marathon	56 km	Saturday of the Easter weekend	621 metres	Cape Town, South Africa
London 2 Brighton Challenge	100 km	May	1500 metres	Richmond, West London/ Brighton

Anthony Rogan

Name of race	Distance	Approx. Date	Elevation (Approx.)	Place of race
Badwater 135	135 miles	July	4450 metres	Death Valley, California
Ultra-Trail Gobi Race	400 km	Late September	Not sure	China, south of the Mongolia border
Tromsø Skyrace	57 km	August	4,800 metres	Tromsø, Norway
Glen Coe Skyline	52 km	September	4,750 metres	Scotland
Leadville 100	100 miles	August	15,600 feet	Leadville, Colorado
Tarawera Ultramarathon	100 miles	February	5470 metres	Rotorua, New Zealand
Desert Solstice 24 hour and 100-mile track invitational	24 hours and 100 miles	December	Competed on a track	Phoenix, Arizona
Brazos Bend 100	100 miles	December	600 feet	Needville, Texas
Miwok 100k	100 km	May	11,800 feet	Stinson Beach, California
Vol-State	500 km	July	Not sure	Dorena Landing, Mississippi County, USA
Barkley Marathons	100 miles	Late March or early April	54,200 feet	Tennessee, USA

Name of race	Distance	Approx. Date	Elevation (Approx.)	Place of race
Black Canyon Ultras	100 km	February	5,190 Feet	Spring Valley to New River, Arizona, USA
Cascade Crest 100 Mile Endurance Run	100 miles	August	23,000+ feet	Easton, Washington, USA
Moab 240 Endurance Run	240.3 miles	October	29,467 feet	Moab, Utah, USA
The 4 Deserts Ultramarathon Series	250 km	March to December	Various	Chile, Mongolia, Namibia, Antarctica
Tahoe 200 Endurance Run	205.5 miles	September	40,200 feet	Lake Tahoe, California and Nevada, USA
Bigfoot 200 Endurance Run	206.5 miles	August	12,802 metres	Washington State, USA
Waldo 100k Trail Run	100 km	August	11,000 feet+	Willamette Pass Ski Area, Oregon Cascades, USA
Rocky Raccoon 100 Trail Race	100 miles	February	5,500 feet	Huntsville, Texas, USA
K85 Innsbruck Alpine Trailrun Festival	86.5 km	September	4, 250 metres	Innsbruck, Austria

Anthony Rogan

REFERENCES

Knechtle, B.; Duff, B.; Welzel, U.; Kohler, G., Body Mass and Circumference of Upper Arm Are Associated with Race Performance in Ultra endurance Runners in a Multistage Race—The Isarrun 2006. Research Quarterly for Exercise and Sport 2009, 80 (2), 262-268.

Knechtle, B.; Knechtle, P.; Kohler, G., Upper arm circumference is associated with race performance in ultra-endurance runners. British Journal of Sports Medicine 2008, 42, 295-299.

Kristin Jean Stuempfle & Martin Dean Hoffman (2015) Gastrointestinal distress is common during a 161-km ultramarathon, Journal of Sports Sciences, 33:17, 1814-1821.

Parnell, J.A., Wagner-Jones, K., Madden R.F., Erdman, KA. (2020) Dietary restrictions in endurance runners to mitigate exercise-induced gastrointestinal symptoms. Journal of the International Society of Sports Nutrition. 17:32.

Gut Training for Endurance Athletes with Patrick Wilson | TrainingPeaks

Pettersen SD, Aslaksen PM, Pettersen SA. Pain Processing in Elite and High-Level Athletes Compared to Non-athletes. *Front Psychol.* 2020;11:1908. Published 2020 Jul 28. doi:10.3389/fpsyg.2020.01908

Brace AW, George K, Lovell GP (2020) Mental toughness and self-efficacy of elite ultra-marathon runners. PLoS ONE 15(11): e0241284. https://doi.org/10.1371/journal.pone.0241284

PERSONAL TRAINER, BOXING COACH, AND KEEN ULTRA-runner Anthony Rogan grew up in Birmingham, England, but now lives in the more peaceful region of Cheshire. He is passionate about moving the body and challenging the mind, and is currently studying for a master's degree in counselling and psychotherapy. This is his first book, and he hopes, through great stories, it inspires others to move their bodies and explore the outdoors.

Printed in Great Britain
by Amazon